I've got bad news, America: normal stink̲ ̲T̲h̲ ̲ ̲n̲o̲r̲m̲a̲l̲ family is broke, stressed, overworked, and generally unhappy. I   ilies, faith, and finances, we've got to stop str   ̲eird!

D0949096

— DAVE RA   HOW;
                    A   OVER

Craig Groeschel is the weirdest person I've ever known. And once you've read this book, you'll understand that's the highest compliment I could ever pay him. Groeschel's passion for God, integrity, and wisdom are abnormal. He approaches his relationship with God on a level that compels all of us to go higher. And it's these very distinctions that make him the perfect person to help you stand apart from a world that is dying in a sea of normalcy. I can't recommend *Weird* highly enough.

— STEVEN FURTICK, SENIOR PASTOR OF ELEVATION CHURCH;
AUTHOR OF *SUN STAND STILL*

Craig Groeschel has always been different in a good sort of way. His new book will motivate you to abandon the normal path and live for Jesus with all your heart.

— JENTEZEN FRANKLIN, PASTOR OF FREE CHAPEL;
AUTHOR OF *FASTING*

This book is nothing at all normal. It's weird. And weird is good. Groeschel's challenge is a timely one, motivating us to jump off the normal path, onto one that may seem weird. As followers of Jesus, we should be different and set apart from the culture around us, to live lives that stand out, never settling for normal again. Since normal is a long way from what God ever intended for us, it's time to turn up the weird! Thanks, Craig, for laying a framework for getting back to what God has called us to.

— BRAD LOMENICK, EXECUTIVE DIRECTOR OF CATALYST

Normal doesn't work! Normal has never accomplished anything significant. And Jesus didn't die on a cross so that his followers could live normal lives. Craig Groeschel does an amazing job of challenging us to go beyond others' expectations in order to honor the calling that Jesus has placed on our lives. Jesus was a lot of things, but normal wasn't one of them. Craig challenges all of us to stop being normal.

— PERRY NOBLE, SENIOR PASTOR OF NEWSPRING CHURCH

Weird is weird. In this book, Craig Groeschel will take your normal life and ask deeper existential questions, leaving you yearning to be weird. No platitudinous easy solutions — rather, an inner view of your life that leads to living off the beaten path. Weird is what we don't know, do, or understand. That's the quest *Weird* will take you on. Go be weird.

— DR. SAMUEL CHAND, INTERNATIONAL SPEAKER, CONSULTANT, AND AUTHOR OF *CRACKING YOUR CHURCH'S CULTURE CODE*

Craig Groeschel is weird in the best kind of way. If anyone can give advice on how to be set apart from the world and just plain weird for God, it's him. His book is a must-read.

— CHRISTINE CAINE, DIRECTOR OF EQUIP AND EMPOWER MINISTRIES; AUTHOR OF *THE CORE ISSUE*

Normal is overrated. *Weird* is inspirational, challenging, and practical.

— ED YOUNG, SENIOR PASTOR OF SECOND BAPTIST HOUSTON

I can't put this book down! I started reading *Weird*, only to realize this book is reading me. It confirms the inner voice that keeps telling me it's time to abandon normal, because normal's not working.

— BIL CORNELIUS, FOUNDING AND LEAD PASTOR OF BAY AREA FELLOWSHIP; AUTHOR OF *I DARE YOU TO CHANGE*

WEIRD

Because normal isn't working.

CRAIG GROESCHEL

ZONDERVAN®

ZONDERVAN.com/
AUTHORTRACKER
follow your favorite authors

We want to hear from you. Please send your comments about this book to us in care of zreview@zondervan.com. Thank you.

ZONDERVAN

Weird
Copyright © 2011 by Craig Groeschel

This title is also available as a Zondervan ebook. Visit www.zondervan.com/ebooks.

This title is also available in a Zondervan audio edition. Visit www.zondervan.fm.

Requests for information should be addressed to:

Zondervan, *Grand Rapids, Michigan 49530*

This edition: ISBN 978-0-310-31576-6 (softcover)

Library of Congress Cataloging-in-Publication Data

Groeschel, Craig.
    Weird : because normal isn't working / Craig Groeschel.
        p.   cm.
    ISBN 978-0-310-32790-5 (hardcover)
    1. Christian life. I. Title.
BV4501.3.G757 2011
    248.4—dc22   2010047194

This book is dedicated to
everyone who is sick of normal
and is ready for something better

Contents

Acknowledgments

To all my friends who offered support, encouragement, and assistance on this project, I'm more grateful than you'll ever know.

I'm especially indebted to:

Dudley Delffs: You are an editing genius. No one can set a table like you.

Tom Dean, Brian Phipps, Sarah Johnson, Curt Diepenhorst, and the whole team at Zondervan: I love your commitment to excellence in Christ-centered publishing.

Brannon Golden: Thanks for your brilliant work on the front end of this project. You and Kendra mean more to me than you know.

Tom Winters: You made a huge difference on this project. Thanks for believing in it.

Lori Tapp: Thank you for keeping me organized and sane at the office. You are an answer to prayer.

Catie, Mandy, Anna, Sam, Bookie, and Joy: You mean everything to me!

Amy: Thanks for being weird with me. You are my dream girl forever.

Introduction

WHY I LOVE
BEING WEIRD

*Know what's weird? Day by day, nothing seems to change.
But pretty soon, everything's different.*

— BILL WATTERSON

From as early as I could remember, my life was pretty normal. As a child, I tattled on my sister, had a crush on the girl next door, and performed Evel Knievel stunts on my red 1975-model Schwinn bike with the fire-striped banana seat. Normal stuff for a kid, right?

In middle school, I enjoyed playing soccer with my friends, watching reruns of *Happy Days*, and playing truth or dare with girls behind the library during recess. Again, pretty normal stuff.

In high school, I ran for student government, counted down the days until I got my driver's license, and exaggerated to my friends about what

I did on dates with the girls I used to meet behind the library. Typical teenage stuff.

In college, I regularly overslept my 8:00 a.m. economics class, charged dozens of Domino's pizzas on my first credit card, and became a brother of Lambda Chi Alpha fraternity. Although I wouldn't have acknowledged it then, looking back I see that being normal was my main goal. Fitting in felt infinitely better than standing out. I worked hard to dress like the rest (Levi's and polos were king), act like the rest (party hearty, study hardly, and in between chase any girl I meet), blend in like the rest (act cool no matter what, talk like everyone else so they'll know I'm as cool as they are).

For me and my peers, normal was in. Nobody we knew wanted to be weird. (Except for that freshman we paid ten dollars to eat a live roach, but I think he liked the notoriety.) Normal was cool, and weird was uncool. Normal people were winners on their way up; weird people were losers headed downward.

When your full-time job is fitting in, you rarely stop to contemplate the more serious issues of life — that is, until one of the more serious issues in life smacks you upside the head. All of us cool-wannabes experienced such a blow one warm October night my sophomore year. Laura, one of the most normal girls I knew, had started driving the three-hour trip home to see her parents. Like most normal college kids, she'd probably had much less sleep — between late weeknights studying and late weekends partying — than her body needed. And on that tragic night, she fell asleep at the wheel, wrapped her car around a tree, and died instantly.

Suddenly normal life didn't seem so normal anymore.

Laura's death was so sudden, so unexpected, and so permanent. She was eighteen and had her whole life ahead of her. Beautiful, smart, funny, she was just like all the rest of us. Only now she had a firm grasp on the meaning of eternity, something my normal friends and I conveniently avoided considering.

Our school hosted a "celebration service" to honor Laura's life and to give us an opportunity to mourn. I sat silently on the end of the third-row pew in that tiny campus chapel most of us had worked so hard to avoid until then, aware that life was now different, but not exactly sure how. Suddenly my English lit test and tennis match the next day no longer seemed so important.

This was only the beginning. Without warning, my normal mindset started to bother me. Like a dull toothache that begins to throb, my discomfort with "the way things were" seemed to increase steadily. For years I'd asked the questions normal people ask: *Why won't the head cheerleader go out with me? What class should I take? Should I change my major? Am I popular enough? Good enough? Successful enough? Can I get a good-enough education to land a good job and afford a good house and marry a good woman and have good kids, all so I can ... what? Be normal?*

With a kind of magnetic power, Laura's death now pulled me toward bigger questions: *Is this all there is to life? Why am I here? What if that had been me dozing off behind the steering wheel? If my life ended now, would it matter? What happens after you die? Is there really a God and a heaven and a hell and all the Christian stuff I've heard about?*

These new questions led me to do something totally abnormal for my frat pack of jocks and hardcore party people: start a Bible study. I admit that, fueled mostly by my newfound fear and anxiety, I also saw an opportunity to improve our fraternity's free-falling reputation. And if I could pass off my new interest in God as a PR move, then my real motivation could remain secret. After all, normal people don't go around thinking about dying and eternity and the meaning of life every day, do they?

And technically, it probably shouldn't have been called a Bible *study*. This was more of a "try to read the Bible with a bunch of people who don't know squat about the Bible" meeting. And for the record, I wasn't the Bible study type. While I wasn't sure what that type was, it seemed a safe bet that it wasn't the guy who hit on sorority girls at the weekly keg party.

So despite the jeering and mocking of our friends, a few frat brothers and I gathered on a Tuesday night in a room affectionately called the Pit to attempt something none of us had ever done alone, much less together: read the Bible.

We started in Matthew chapter 1 (I knew enough to start with the New Testament and not Genesis) and plowed forward the best we could. At the end of each gathering, we'd pray and ask God to keep us safe while we partied the upcoming weekend. Kind of different, I know. But that's where we were at the time.

This Bible study attempt foreshadowed even more weirdness. Strangely enough, the more I read the Bible, the more it felt like God was starting to speak to me. Each day I read something that seemed especially personal and timely — words of encouragement or conviction or forgiveness. Gradually my heart started to warm toward God. Maybe he was real after all. Experiencing his voice through Scripture, I sensed he was gently drawing me, calling me, pulling me.

As the spiritual tug continued to strengthen its grip, I started to contemplate what taking God seriously would mean. *What if Jesus is real? What if his teachings are true? How would my life change if I truly tried to live like Jesus? What if I really gave my life to God?*

Although I didn't know all the answers, I knew enough to foresee that pursuing my new questions would force me to step outside the safe circle of being normal.

RED-LETTER WEIRD

As I dived into my new passion for Bible study, I noticed that certain words were printed in red and not black — the words of Jesus. As if what he was saying didn't stand out enough! When I read what Jesus taught, it was anything but normal. His teachings were so weird that they could easily be considered otherworldly.

Jesus said, "Love your enemies, do good to those who hate you, bless those who curse you, pray for those who mistreat you. If someone strikes you on one cheek, turn to him the other also" (Luke 6:27 – 29).

Normal says to hate your enemies. Jesus says to love them.

Normal seeks revenge on those who hurt you. Jesus shows you how to be kind to those who harm you.

If someone hits you, then normal swings back. Jesus teaches you to turn the other cheek.

Let's be honest. This is not only counterintuitive to everything we learned on the playground in elementary school; it's just downright weird. And these are not the most challenging of his unusual teachings. Jesus also told us to pray for those who persecute us. *Weird.* And if we want to find our lives, we have to lose them. *Weirder.* And if we don't hate our parents, we really aren't committed to him. *Weirdest.*

Preparing for our weekly "try to read the Bible with a bunch of people who don't know squat about the Bible" meeting, I ran into two verses like a brick wall: "Enter through the narrow gate. For wide is the gate and broad is the road that leads to destruction, and many enter through it. But small is the gate and narrow the road that leads to life, and only a few find it" (Matt. 7:13 – 14).

These red-yelling words of Jesus struck me full force. *Many* are on the road to destruction. *Few* are on the road to life. Where was I? Was I driving with the flow of traffic racing blindly down the wrong highway? Or was I heading in the right direction along with a few others down a one-lane road?

Although I wanted to believe I was one of the few, my heart knew I was stuck in a traffic jam. Jesus' words screamed like a big neon sign, pointing out a route that I had failed to notice as I tried to keep up with the convoy of normalcy. The truth of his words suddenly seemed so clear.

The majority of people — the crowd — is traveling the wrong path, the one that leads to destruction. They're the normal ones — intent on looking like the rest, spending money like the rest, living like the rest, keeping up with the rest. But their road leads to a dead end. Only a few people — the weird ones unafraid to exit the normal highway — find the right road. Not many, but a small and brave group of travelers willing to separate from the crowd and embark on a different kind of journey down a less obvious path.

Talk about a major U-turn! Here I was, comfortably cruising down the interstate at eighty miles per hour, assuming I was headed in the right direction since everyone else was going the same way, when suddenly the GPS revealed that where I *really* wanted to go was in the opposite direction on a small back road. To really follow Jesus, to know him, meant that I'd have to be different from my friends and everyone else. But I didn't want to be different, one of those goofy Christians I'd seen around campus with their guitars and clever little tracts that weren't supposed to look like tracts. Christians were different and different was weird and I was committed to being normal.

And since I didn't want to be weird, I wasn't about to change my course and follow Jesus.

WEIRD 101

Who could blame me? Tell the truth: Haven't you noticed how weird Christians can be? You know what I'm talking about. That late-night, low-budget, cable-access Christian television weird. Not just big hair (being from Oklahoma, I'm used to that) but also big *purple* hair. Pronouncing *Jesus* with the violent inflection of a carnival barker: "Jeee-*zuss*! Be healed in the name of Jeee-*zuss!*" Wearing suits in cartoon-character colors and promising God's blessing in exchange for a monthly "contribution."

As I continued to wrestle with the conviction I experienced in reading Jesus' words, I was forced to rethink weird. What if being the Christian kind of weird did not mean the same thing as the bad-weird, freak-show, annoying, carnival-barking, somewhat uncomfortable, weird-for-no-reason weird? What if the Bible is talking about a different-than-what-everyone-else-does, good type of Jesus weird?

Although I had always believed in God, I had to acknowledge that I didn't really know him or what it meant to follow him. Maybe the weird I associated with religious people wasn't how he intended Christians to be different. Maybe there was a whole new wild world of weird that came with choosing the narrow path. Maybe it was time to abandon the normal and wide path I'd known and off-road it for a wonderful weirdness I couldn't imagine.

After a Tuesday night Bible meeting, I walked alone to an empty softball field. No matter what it cost me — even being normal — I had decided that I wanted to know Jesus and live for him. I wanted to do life his way and not mine. As I knelt beside the dugout and prayed, I left normal behind and embraced whatever it took — being different to the point of the God kind of weird — to follow Jesus. Something melted within me, and I walked away forever changed, with a sense of God's grace I can't describe.

It didn't take long for others to notice the change. When I told my fraternity brothers and teammates that I'd become a Christian, they gazed at me with the tentative uncertainty usually reserved for wild animals and mental patients. They quickly realized, however, that I wasn't dangerous — just weird. In a matter of moments, I'd gone from a cool, normal, somewhat popular, regular kind of guy to a first-class Jesus freak.

Perhaps the most immediately noticeable change was my commitment to purity — no more sex until marriage. To say the least, my sex-obsessed buddies thought I had really lost it and had drunk more than my share of the bad Kool-Aid. Several frat guys even wagered a hundred dollars that I wouldn't last one month without going back to my old ways. For the record, they lost their money!

NORMAL'S NOT WORKING

I grew to love being the God kind of weird so much that a couple of years later I became a pastor. (Some of you are thinking, "Now, that's *really* weird!") And during this time, I've seen a lot of normal people — some seemingly working harder at it than others. They're everywhere; even today, when everyone wants to be recognized as an individual, they're still wanting to be accepted for fitting in.

However, nowadays being normal isn't quite as easy and painless as it once seemed to be. In fact, it's more time consuming than ever. There aren't enough hours in the day to buy, sell, drive, cook, clean, call, shop, eat, plan, study, write, review, schedule, and follow through on everything. Overwhelmed, overloaded, and exhausted, everybody talks about wanting more time, but only to "catch up" on what they're already doing — rushing, planning, worrying, and rushing some more. Families suffer. Health wanes. Priorities fade. Joy evaporates. Most people don't know their life's direction because their soul is dizzy from spinning around so much. Uninterrupted time to rest, relax, and enjoy life sounds like a line from a retirement home brochure. Normal is busy and getting busier.

When it comes to finances, it's normal to go into debt so deep that you can't see the way out. Money becomes a dark pit of worry, fear, anxiety, tension, and fighting. Most people I know are living paycheck to paycheck. Most make more money today than they ever have, but it's never enough. Now more than ever, it's expensive to be normal — so much cool stuff to buy and take care of, so many normal experiences you want your family to have. Only it's hard to enjoy any of it when the financial noose tightens with each monthly payment.

Normal relationships require little and provide less. You and your spouse are so busy, so stressed, and so exhausted, there's normally no time for each other. No wonder, then, that affairs are the norm. They provide the attention, romance, and sex without the commitment, sacrifice, or intimacy required in marriage. Similarly, you'd love to spend more time with the kids, but there's just not enough time. They're almost as busy and stressed as you are. It would be great to have deep, meaningful conversations and shared experiences that allow you to teach them what you know. Normal families, however, just don't work that way.

And nothing's more normal than sex, right? Premarital sex, extramarital sex, friends-with-benefits type sex. Porn, experimentation, casual hookups — whatever feels good between consenting adults. It's totally normal. Maybe our parents were uptight and repressed about sex, but we're more progressive, more liberated nowadays. In the twenty-first century, why in the world would anyone remain a virgin until marriage? After all, as one of my frat brothers used to say, "You wouldn't buy the car without test driving it first, would you?" Unfortunately, though, normal also carries a hefty price: guilt, shame, confusion, remorse, disease, addiction, unwanted children, and divorce.

Normal infects our faith as well, both what we believe and how we live it out. When we consider how people relate to God, it's normal to either reject God altogether or believe in him while living as if he doesn't exist. In churches, normal is lukewarm Christianity, self-centered spiritual consumerism, and shallow, me-driven faith. God has become a means to an end, a tool in our toolbox to accomplish what we want. The majority of people claim to know God, but by their actions they deny him.

And all this is normal.

But normal isn't working.

WEIRD ON PURPOSE

In this book, I'm going to challenge you to jump off the normal path and onto one that may seem a little weird. At times, you're going to argue, "But, Craig — that's just *too* weird!" When that happens, we're likely making progress. We're going to talk about dramatic changes. Because, let's face it, if small changes would've made the difference, you'd have made those changes a long time ago. Everyone travels along the wide road; only a few take the narrow path.

You certainly don't have to agree with all my ideas, but if you take the Bible seriously, I trust you won't deny that the way normal people live today is miles away from what God intended. Separating ourselves from what the world considers normal is not just a matter of obedience. God invites us to dance to a different tune, because he knows what's truly going to satisfy and fulfill us.

Instead of living stressed, overwhelmed, and exhausted, you can live a life of meaningful relationships, intentional scheduling, and deep, fulfilling rest for your soul. Instead of choking with constant financial fear and tension, you can let God's Word lead you along a path to financial peace, margin, and eternal investments. Instead of allowing your marriage to drift into parallel lives or divorce by default, you can experience true intimacy with your spouse. Rather than continuing on the normal sexual path toward pain, emptiness, and idolatry, you can allow God to heal you, change the way you think, and place deliberate safeguards in your life to protect you. God wants you to know him and love him — not just acknowledge him or consider him a cosmic sugar daddy.

If you let him, if you choose not to coast along the world's wide-open road but rather to blaze a narrow trail with Jesus as your guide, then you'll never settle for normal again. You'll want only one thing.

The God kind of weird.

Part One

TIME

Chapter 1

KILLING TIME

When you kill time, remember that it has no resurrection.

— A. W. Tozer

J ust before Christmas, my whole family piled into our kid-moving vehicle and rushed to the nearest mall to grab some last-minute Christmas presents before dashing to a holiday party. As usual, we were running late and were slightly on edge.

Entering the mall parking lot, I was overwhelmed by the traffic. Cars crawled bumper to bumper, inching along like a million ants trapped in a puddle of honey. Instinctively I prayed one of those selfish "God, please get me a parking space" prayers (as if God wants me to get one before all the other ants). Out of the corner of my eye, I spotted an old pickup truck near the mall entrance, leaving its space. *God is so good.* I punched the accelerator and sped toward my answered prayer, hoping to gain a few precious extra seconds.

I immediately staked my spot with eye-lock. (Eye-lock is the ancient practice of claiming a spot by looking directly at it. As long as you don't look away, the spot is yours.) Relieved that I might actually avoid the tedium of trolling up and down each aisle, I kept my eyes deadlocked on the spot and prepared for entry. Out of nowhere, a red sports car whipped in front of me — breaking my honorable eye-lock — and stole *my* parking space.

Unbelievable.

Frustrated beyond words, with the pressure mounting because of our tight schedule, I did something that I'm not proud of doing. While my wife pleaded with me and my kids prayed loudly, I backed up my vehicle, pointed it directly at the red sports car, shifted to neutral, then revved my engine.

The driver of the sports car glanced into his rearview mirror, only to see me glaring at him. Like a drag racer leaving the gate, I popped from neutral to drive, peeled out, and shot straight toward the rear of the enemy car.

It's hard to know what happened next. Maybe it was my wife threatening me. Perhaps God answered my kids' prayers. Maybe I realized that I was still in our minivan and not in a NASCAR race. Whatever the reason, right before impact, I slammed on the brakes and stopped just short of his car. With all the Christian love I had, I rolled down the window and shouted at the top of my lungs, "What do you think you're doing? You know I had eye-lock, you idiot! Now you're going to make me really late, you red-sports-car-driving loser!"

After rejoining the other ants, we searched for another twenty minutes and finally found a parking spot somewhere near the state line. Thanks to me, no one in my family had the Christmas spirit as we entered the mall (my wife barely speaking to me), running even more behind schedule. We dashed from store to store, breathing heavy in our rush. As we entered JC Penney, who should approach us but my old friend — the driver of the red car.

Just great. Images of my picture with the headline "Local Pastor Assaults Man over Parking Space" flashed through my mind.

"I can tell you're in a big hurry," he said, as my blood pressure continued to rise. "But it appears you have more going on in your life than you can handle." My wife gave me the remember-you're-a-pastor-and-better-behave look as the driver continued. "I'd like to tell you about someone who could really help — Jesus. I really believe you need him, and he could change your life."

Ouch.

WHEN MORE ISN'T BETTER

I can't blame my lack of self-control on our culture, but it surely doesn't help any of us manage our time well. We live in a time-starved society that relentlessly pushes us to the limits — and not just at the holidays. Buy more, do more, accomplish more, conquer more. Rush, rush. Hurry, hurry. More productive, more efficient, more expedient — more, more, more. It's insane what passes for the norm today. Most people work far more hours than they used to (who works only forty hours anymore?), trying to get ahead or simply survive. Our evenings or off times are crammed with activities — the kids' sports, music lessons, and, yes, church. Many families rarely have time to eat together. A typical family dinner now includes a round of Happy Meals from the drive-through in the fifteen minutes between dance and soccer practice.

Even kids are overwhelmed today. I know many families with seven- and eight-year-old kids who, on top of homework and school, are out four or five nights a week doing extracurriculars (not to mention the schedule

they have to keep on the weekends). And in our culture this is normal —
or even expected. We all want our kids to be well-rounded, don't we?
We wouldn't want to deprive them of the lifestyle necessities that their
friends have, would we?

You have enough time to do everything God wants you to do.

For many of us, the schedules we impose on our children end up consuming us. If someone asked, "Are you really enjoying your life?" most of us would have to say, "No ... and I don't have time to talk about it!"

We're always rushed, always on the move, never having enough time. Almost everyone I know has little room for error in their schedule. Tragically, most people have little time for the things in life that they would say are the most important to them. When we overschedule ourselves in the belief that we can do everything, we stop being human and try to become godlike — not only impossible but also incredibly arrogant. Most of us are living at a pace that is not only unsustainable; it's also unbiblical.

Instead of our typical conclusion that we simply don't have enough time, what if we embraced the truth — no matter how weird or counterintuitive it might seem?

You have enough time to do everything God wants you to do.

God has given you everything you need to accomplish all that he wants you to do, including enough time (see 2 Peter 1:3). We don't need more time. We need to use the time we already have differently. You have time for what you choose to invest your time in. Every day most of us say, "I just don't have time to work out ... to read the Bible ... to go to church this week ... to meet for lunch ... to add one more thing." But the truth is, we find time for what's important to us. If golf is really a priority to us, we find time to play golf. If going to dinner with our friends matters, we make it happen. If tanning, working out, or getting our hair cut is a priority, we seem to find time. Catch yourself the next time you're about to say, "I don't have time" for something. Tell yourself the truth: either it's not a priority and you're guarding your time for good reason, or you simply aren't willing to choose to spend your time on it.

Normal people do normal things at a normal — breakneck — pace and never have enough time to do the most important things. This is why we are called to buck the trend of accelerating busyness and reset our race engines to God's speed. Fueled by faith and passion for our true priorities, we're going to drive against traffic in order to find rest, refreshment, and time for what matters most in life.

A TALE OF TWO SISTERS

Our constant busyness is causing us to miss more than just rest and refreshment. I'm convinced normal people miss the majority of God's blessings because they're too busy to notice them. Nowhere is this more apparent than in a scene of two women at odds over how they're each spending their time. One is convinced she doesn't have enough time; her sister, however, accepts an opportunity for a unique encounter and, as a result, receives a gift with literally eternal payoff: "As Jesus and his disciples were on their way, he came to a village where a woman named Martha opened her home to him. She had a sister called Mary, who sat at the Lord's feet listening to what he said. But Martha was distracted by all the preparations that had to be made" (Luke 10:38 – 40).

Here's what's interesting: Mary and Martha are both presented with the same opportunity. Jesus, the very Son of God, has come to Martha's home. What would *you* do if you knew Jesus was coming over? Now, Mary probably had other things she needed to do, just like the rest of us. Maybe she had laundry that wasn't done. She might have needed to go buy some groceries (or kill the fatted calf — talk about a time drainer).

Certainly she could have swept, cleaned, and tidied up. But she chose to create a moment instead. She said, "Right now, while we have this time, I'm not going to do any of that other stuff. I'm going to seize this moment and simply enjoy being with Jesus while I can."

Mary made a deliberate choice. She wasn't being lazy and using company as an excuse to get out of helping her sister with chores. She was choosing to focus on what mattered the most.

When's the last time you stopped long enough to embrace a matters-the-most moment?

If you're like me, it takes a few reminders. Just last night I was sitting in my home office replying to emails. My youngest daughter, Joy, bounced in to see me. With her long hair pulled back in pigtails and her mouth smudged with Oreo crumbs, she asked, "Dad, can we play a game?"

Lost in my work, I mumbled the Busy Parent's Creed: "In a minute, honey ... I'm doing something important ... Let me finish my work ... We'll see ... Maybe later."

Without missing a beat, Joy blurted out, "Daddy, look at me and *never* forget this. I'm only going to be six years old once! You don't want to miss it!"

I smiled at her negotiation tactic — kid guilt works every time. Nonetheless, my all-important work didn't seem so urgent anymore. I gladly closed the computer, stuffed an Oreo in my mouth, and sat down for an epic game of Go Fish.

It's so tempting to let these moments pass us by because we're overwhelmed by everything clamoring for our attention. The task-driven Martha knew this too well. While Mary embraced the moment, Martha, on the other hand, was like many of us: preoccupied, distracted, busy being busy. Martha was wigging out, she was freaking, she was losing it.

And here's the kicker: the distractions consuming Martha weren't bad things. She wasn't bent on doing evil. She wasn't enticed by the pursuit of something sinful. In fact, we might even say that her priorities were good and necessary. In all fairness to Martha, we might be thinking along the same lines if we were in her place: "Okay, I gotta think this through. This is Jesus coming over. *The* Jesus. Everybody's saying he's the Son of God, the Christ! I'd better get out the pretty Pottery Barn china with the little sparrows and fig leaves. I'm going to need new candles. I've got to make sure the toilet paper matches the shower curtain. I certainly want the Lord to have a good impression of our home and family — God forbid that we look like a bunch of pagans!"

Sound familiar? Just like Martha, we fall into the trap of being busy instead of being bigger than the tyranny of the urgent. I've heard it said, "If the Devil can't make us really bad, then he'll try to make us really busy." Absolutely true. What's most important is often not what seems most urgent. When something small loudly demands all our attention, its noise often drowns out the whisper of what's enormously important.

> "If the Devil can't make us really bad, then he'll try to make us really busy."

Martha becomes so intent on her mission that she can't imagine why anyone else wouldn't be doing the same things. Consider the urgency in her voice: "Lord, don't you care that my sister has left me to do the work by myself? Tell her to help me!" (Luke 10:40). However, she's not hearing her own message. Martha tells Jesus with her lips that he's the most important thing ("Lord"), even as she's absolutely convinced that all this activity is the *right* thing to do. "Jesus, I'm doing all this work — making drinks with the little umbrellas, preparing special hors d'oeuvres (gluten free, with no bacon), unloading the dishwasher, staging the dinner table — and Mary's just lying around shooting the breeze! Are you kidding me?" Martha not only misses the opportunity before her; she feels more than justified in missing it.

MAJORITY RULES

Mary and Martha's dilemma is the challenge for all of us. Most of us are convinced that the way we're already living is absolutely necessary ... and right. Our culture, the world we live in, has brainwashed us: "This is the way we *have* to live! Being really busy means you're successful, important, and significant." We become convinced that this standard — lots of "important" activity, the business of busyness — is what truly matters, an indication of our talent, worth, and value. Anybody worth anything will always be busy, right?

In the introduction, I mentioned the eye-opening effect that Matthew 7:13 had on me at a crucial time in my life. Let's look at it again, from a different version of the Bible. "The highway to hell is broad, and its gate is wide for the many who choose that way" (NLT). Everybody's doing it! Well, if it seems like *everybody's* doing it, then clearly they're on a broad path. They're going through a wide gate. Many are choosing that way, because the bandwagon requires a huge exit ramp to accommodate all its passengers.

Notice that these verses start with "You can enter God's Kingdom only through the narrow gate," then continues, "The gateway to life is very narrow and the road is difficult, and only a few ever find it" (Matt. 7:13 – 14 NLT). So if it seems like you're doing something different from what everyone else is doing, and if sometimes that feels hard, this is a good thing, not a bad thing.

When I compare the pace of my life with the rhythm of God's Word, it quickly becomes apparent I'm doing something wrong. Just because everyone else is doing something doesn't make it right. (Wow, I just said something my mom told me for years.) In fact, when everyone else is doing it, it begs for scrutiny. Instead of just naturally following the herd instinct and doing what everyone else is doing, what if we automatically

Normal people allow good things to become the enemy of the best things.

questioned the majority rule? Again, like Martha wanting to present Jesus with a lovely meal in a beautiful setting, there may be nothing inherently wrong with popular behavior. It may even be a good thing. But is it the best thing?

Normal people allow good things to become the enemy of the best things.

Too many good (or acceptable) things quickly overwhelm the most important things in life. Too often our desire to fit in, to belong, to conform and be considered normal eclipses our desire to follow God and do what's best. We choose popular standards instead of the habits that lead to holiness.

In his letter to the Romans, Paul tells us exactly how we can counter this: "Do not conform any longer to the pattern of this world, but be transformed by the renewing of your mind" (Rom. 12:2). What makes us think that public opinion knows what's best? What gives the majority the authority to determine what's right?

If we follow Christ, we're not supposed to be like everyone else. The whole point of sanctification is to become more like him instead of who we are when left to our own devices and desires. So how do we discern the difference between a good choice and the best one?

Paul provides the answer with the second part of this verse. "Do not conform any longer to the pattern of this world, but be transformed by the renewing of your mind. *Then you will be able to test and approve what God's will is — his good, pleasing and perfect will*" (emphasis mine).

YOUR TO-DON'T LIST

Imagine meeting someone for the first time, and after making small talk, you politely ask, "What kind of work do you do?" Your new acquaintance replies, "I don't do much at all; I usually just hang out at home and wait for friends to drop by." What would you think? Most of us tend to look down on people who don't produce visible results and demonstrate their accomplishments. Why? Because we usually equate busyness with importance. This isn't just about worldly accomplishments; it's about spiritual worth as well.

One of the foundational lies we've absorbed about the value of busyness is that it indicates our spiritual worth. If we work hard and get our lives together and do as many good and valuable things as possible, then God will be pleased. And since he wants us to have our lives together, then he must want us to keep working until we figure out how to get everything in our lives just right. This sounds right, doesn't it?

Wrong. Most normal people believe that God will never give us more than we can handle. The problem is, God never said that. He said he would not let you be tempted without a way out (see 1 Cor. 10:13), but he never said he wouldn't give you more than you can handle. Ready for a weird take on this?

Just because we can do something doesn't mean we should.

God will often give you more than you can handle so you can learn to depend on him rather than on yourself.

If you could handle everything yourself, you wouldn't need God. Moses certainly learned this the hard way. Like many normal people today, he was overwhelmed with more responsibilities than one man could handle. As a leader of millions, he spent his whole day solving literally hundreds of problems. He finally became so overwhelmed, he cried out to God to take his life. In Numbers 11:16 – 17, God said to Moses, "Bring me seventy of Israel's elders ... and I will take of the Spirit that is on you and put the Spirit on them. They will *help you carry the burden* of the people so that you will not have to *carry it alone*" (emphasis mine).

If you have more than you can handle, God wants you to lean on him to lighten your load. You don't have to do it all, and God doesn't expect you to do it all alone. All the more reason to allow him to guide your decisions about your workload, schedule, and commitments. We must discern what God calls us to accomplish rather than mindlessly adding on everything presented to us.

When you go to an all-you-can-eat buffet, it's tempting to fill three plates, because everything looks so good and it's all included in one low price. There's fried chicken, grilled steak, mashed potatoes, glazed carrots, creamed broccoli, green beans, sweet potatoes, fruit salad, green Jell-O, warm dinner rolls (with honey butter), chocolate pie, and strawberry shortcake. But if you load up on everything available, someone will have to load you into an ambulance!

You have to make some choices, both to savor what you do eat as well as to maintain your health. Similarly, each day you may be tempted to bite off way more than you can chew. We have to remind ourselves that just because we can do something doesn't mean we should.

Or think of it another way. If you're around my age, you might remember the old theme song to *Schoolhouse Rock*'s "Conjunction Junction." You remember: "Conjunction Junction, what's your function?" (Ah, pop culture. If you don't have a clue what I'm talking about, you can pause and give thanks to God.) One of the most important things we can do in life to combat busyness is change our conjunction.

Instead of saying "and," we need to learn to say "or."

Instead of fried chicken *and* grilled steak, we can have fried chicken *or* grilled steak. Instead of soccer practice *and* guitar lessons, you and your child can pick soccer *or* guitar. Instead of working late *and* taking work home, it's one *or* the other.

For example, right now in my life, on top of leading the church, writing this book, and ministering to pastors, I would also like to start an inner-city ministry *and* play in a soccer league *and* coach my kids' football team *and* serve on the board of the local homeless shelter *and* still have time with my kids. All good things and totally normal. But if I want to stay on the narrow path, I'm going to have to focus more deliberately. Which means reminding myself that, in addition to my normal duties, I could start an inner-city ministry *or* play in a soccer league *or* coach my kids' football team *or* serve on the board *or* spend time with my kids. Keeping an "or" in the water prevents filling your boat with so many good things that they ultimately sink the ship.

While normal people continue to add items to their to-do list, maybe you should do something weird instead: start a to-don't list. Just this year alone, I've dropped seven things that I normally do to make room for those important things I thought I didn't have time to do. I'd like to challenge you to stop reading and start your to-don't list. Maybe you should do something weird and write down at least three activities in your life that you're going to drop. Put something down and let it go.

> **While normal people continue to add items to their to-do list, maybe you should do something weird instead: start a to-don't list.**

WEIRD STANDARD TIME

Why do so many of us live jam-packed lives? Why do we plan to slow down one day but then never actually do it? Why do we remain so busy even as we complain about it and experience its constant erosion of our quality of life?

Will you have anything to show for all the busyness, competitions, and activities besides ribbons, trophies, worn-out ballet shoes, and a hard drive full of pictures? How many world-class athletes retire with countless trophies but no family? How many entrepreneurs have a stellar 401(k) but don't know their kid's GPA? Or, as Jesus put it so clearly, how many people gain the whole world but lose their souls (Luke 9:25)?

If you're constantly burdened by the weight of all the many chores, tasks, responsibilities, obligations, and commitments in your life, then it's time to change. It's time to create a margin in which you can not only focus on your true priorities but also simply breathe and begin to enjoy life again. If killing time is killing you, then keep reading.

The next two chapters will examine the best ways I know for unplugging the busy machine that's constantly tailgating our lives. First, we'll look at practicing the power of being present. Which sounds a lot cooler, hipper, New Age, and Zen than I intend, because what I'm talking about, as you'll see, is simply a fundamental awareness of God's presence in each moment of our lives.

The second area is one you may know but don't practice regularly: taking a Sabbath. Notice I said "taking" instead of "observing" the Sabbath. Knowing how to rest, to unplug, to unwind is as much a spiritual discipline as prayer or fasting. As weird as it may sound, God *commands* us to rest. It's not an option to keep going at the pace, intensity, and speed at which most of us live our lives.

Busyness will remain the standard for many people for years to come. But we're called to a different standard, a way of prioritizing our time that may seem weird to everyone around us. When we follow Jesus, we're about our Father's business, not about the world's busyness.

Check your watch. It's time to get weird.

Chapter 2

NO TIME LIKE THE PRESENT

You must live in the present, launch yourself on every wave, find your eternity in each moment.

— HENRY DAVID THOREAU

While in a restaurant recently, I noticed a family of four eating together. My first thought was, "How nice! It's so great to see a family enjoying some time together." When I glanced their way again, each person's head was bowed, and I assumed they were praying before their meal. But when they kept looking down, I realized: all of them were typing into their phones! They were oblivious to one another, each person focused instead on connecting with people who weren't even there. You've probably witnessed a similar scene — it may even have been your own family!

It's not just texting and playing on our iGadgets that's diverting our attention. According to Nielsen, the average person spends twenty-eight hours in front of their television each week. This is in addition to the sixteen hours a week, on average, that we spend in front of our computers.[1] No wonder then that orthopedists see over twenty-two million people a year for thumb injuries caused by texting! Okay, I totally just made up that last one, but I'm convinced God intended more than texting and hitchhiking when he gave us opposable thumbs.

It's not just busyness that's clogging our schedules and preventing us from enjoying the fullness of life as God intended. Maybe it's a chicken-or-egg situation, but I believe that the consequence of busyness destroys us more than the overwhelming stress of too much to do. As long as we're so busy, our minds and hearts are somewhere else: at work, at home, at the hospital, at the church, on and on. We're simply not present. Our minds are so cluttered with endless to-do lists that there's no room for us to experience the joy in being alive today.

PRESENT AND ACCOUNTED FOR

Right now, even as you read this, how many other thoughts are swimming around in your head? Normally, we all have so much on our minds, so many things to remember and get done. You have a lot going on at your job. You've got the big presentation on Wednesday that you haven't even started yet. How are you going to get it all done? Your kids have homework (including the big science project they've been putting off because you've been putting off a trip to Target for supplies), and they have to be at soccer. Oh yeah, and there's the youth lock-in tomor-

When you are with the people you love, chances are good your mind may not be.

row night. The oil needs changing on your car. Your yard needs mowing, and you need a haircut. You have to buy a wedding present for your friends from your small group. Which reminds you — the outfit you're planning to wear to the wedding needs to go to the cleaners ...

When you are with the people you love, chances are good your mind may not be. In our small group of friends that meets regularly, I asked if this was a problem. Every couple in the room acknowledged this was a challenge for them. The wives in particular explained that even when their husbands were home, their husbands' minds often seemed to be elsewhere.

And I'm as guilty as the next guy. For years this was a normal scenario at our house. Amy would be talking to me about anything. Since my mind was elsewhere, I'd slip into barely acknowledging her with an occasional "Uh-huh." After a few minutes she'd abruptly ask, "Are you listening to me?" Then with survival instincts, I'd quickly (and miraculously) repeat her last few words to prove that I was listening — even though both of us knew she did not have my undivided attention.

Wherever you are, be all there.

My not-all-there problem is not limited to my private thoughts. I can also be at the movies on a date, at a dance recital, or at a family day in the park and still be working on my iPhone. Even though I'm physically present, I'm not mentally or emotionally present. After years of these normal distractions, Amy asked me to do something that seemed to wake me from a long relational nap. With a very understanding spirit, she explained, "I know you have a lot going on with the church. I'll always support you. But when you are with the family, can you be all here?" Her request was simple and more than reasonable.

Wherever you are, be all there.

I'll never try to pretend that I've perfected the art of being present.

Far from it. But I've made drastic improvements. Normal people live distracted, rarely fully present. Weird people silence the distractions and remain fully in the moment. It's an unusual practice that can radically improve your quality of life and the depth of your relationships.

25/8

As we explored in the last chapter, simply having more time is not the answer. While busyness is categorically the norm for the vast majority of people in the Western world, the solution is never about having more time. We know this, but still we forget such an essential truth. People often say to me (and I'm guilty of saying it as well), "I wish there were more hours in the day; if only I had more time!" And why do we want more time? What would we do with it? We want more time to do the important things that aren't getting done. This list might include time to rest, time to spend with God, or simply time to enjoy our families and loved ones.

But let's be honest with ourselves. What if God suddenly said, "I'm giving you one extra hour a day? You now have twenty-five hours in a day?" Or better yet, what if he decided to give us an eighth day of the week — which amounts to over three extra hours each day? How would you spend that time? Would you use it for an afternoon nap or to get caught up on last month's expense report at the office? Would you use it for a meaningful conversation with your spouse or to get the oil changed (finally — only a thousand miles overdue) on your car? Extra prayer and reflection time with God or online surfing for the best deal on that flight for Thanksgiving?

I suspect most of us would spend our new 25/8 time catching up on chores, doing more

The answer isn't more time but a greater awareness of the time we have.

work, or finding long-lost grade school classmates on Facebook. Would you really spend a solid hour in meaningful conversation with your aging grandma or teenage son? Despite good intentions, I'm as likely as the next person to try to get caught up in all the areas where my life seems to be spilling over around the edges.

The answer isn't more time but a greater awareness of the time we have.

It's like a car with wheels that aren't aligned. It always pulls to one side. If you don't constantly fight it, that little tug will drag you right off the road. And the constant battle to keep the vehicle within the lines becomes exhausting. No one wants to drive very far when they're out of alignment.

The culture we live in is forever pulling us off center — go faster, work harder, stay busy. If we don't fight it, we're not only headed for the ditch. We're back on the wide road with everybody else.

TIME OUT

Can you even imagine your life where you have time for the important and not the urgent? When one of your kids is talking to you, do you give them your undivided attention? Or are you also thinking about what to pick up for dinner or the deadline at work tomorrow? When someone interrupts you in the hall at the office, are you glad to talk to them? Or are you annoyed? (Maybe that depends on the person.)

Do you have time to rest? No, I mean *really* rest — an uninterrupted night's sleep, a quiet morning over a cup of coffee as you watch it rain, a stroll along the beach as the waves erase your footprints? When's the last time you got to relax? Do you ever just sit and reflect on your life — without watching the clock, setting the alarm on your iPhone, or becoming distracted by the laundry waiting to be folded?

When you're with the people you love, do you connect intimately and enjoy each other? Or do you exchange essential information ("I thought you already paid the American Express bill!" "Did you stop at the cleaners?" "What time is practice?") that often leads to tension or an outright fight? Do you have plenty of quality time with the Creator of this universe — the one who made you — so that all the other things fall into place? Or are you set on "normal" and usually lacking time for what's most important?

When do you have time to be in the present moment?

If you're feeling troubled by your answers, pulled from the present moment on a regular basis, then consider this admonition: "Be very careful, then, how you live — not as unwise but as *wise*, making the most of every opportunity, because the days are evil. Therefore do not be foolish, but understand what the Lord's will is" (Eph. 5:15 – 17, emphasis mine).

Be wise, not foolish.

Be weird, not normal.

Don't let culture divert you from living in the present, being fully engaged with the people around you and the gifts and challenges that draw you back to God. Don't let the chaotic pace of normalcy tug you in the wrong direction. You'll have to fight against the daily drift — others' expectations, the urgent but unimportant, a false sense of self — or you'll get swept away by a normal life. Be different. Be careful how you live, how you plan: what you say yes to and what you say no to.

Notice the relationship between the choices we make — wise or foolish — and understanding the Lord's will. It's critical to God that we think about how we live, how we spend the present time with which we're gifted each day.

How do you figure out what you should do with your time? In his book *The Best Question Ever*, Andy Stanley offers a simple question you can ask to help you make the best decision in almost any situation. Let's say I asked you, "Hey, do you and your spouse want to go out to dinner with us Friday night?" If we already know each other, most of you would simply check with your spouse and your calendar: "Are we free that night?"

While there's nothing wrong with this question, it's not the best question. Here's a better question to ask: "Is it *wise*?" Stanley explains that you have to know what's important to you, and that determines how you make wise choices — even about such "normal" decisions as whether to have dinner with the pastor and his wife this weekend. In light of everything that you know right now, all your goals, your dreams, where you are in your life, your personal experience, is this the wisest choice you could make? Consider the invitation I offered. If you pause for a moment to consider more than just your availability, then a variety of other variables might come into play:

- You've been attacking debt, so you've cut back on nonessentials like cable TV, buying electronics, and eating out. Knowing that you might have to charge the meal (or at least offer to tip), you decide it would be very unwise to go out.
- You've been working on your marriage. Your spouse has told you he or she wants a regular date night commitment, where just the two of you go somewhere to talk and enjoy being together. You farm the kids out to their friends to spend the night, or enlist relatives to babysit. Since Fridays have been your regular date night, would it be worth sacrificing just to hear Groeschel drone on and on about his upcoming sermon series on Leviticus?
- One or both of you are trying to lose some weight, so you've started exercising and eating more carefully. How likely would it be that you could pass up the strawberry cheesecake if you went out to eat?

Given all these factors, and after further discussion with your spouse, your answer should probably be, "Maybe some other time." (If that's the case, have the courage to tell me no. I'll get over it. I promise.) You have to decide what things are important to you and can help you make decisions. Consider starting to ask, "Is this wise?" with a wise-criteria qualifier tacked onto the front:

> "In light of our future hopes and dreams,..."
> "With our current family situation,..."
> "Because we know our marriage isn't where God wants it to be,..."
> "Since I plan on going to graduate school,..."
> "We have two children in diapers, so ..."
> "Our seventeen-year-old will only be with us for one more year,
> so ..."

Make your own list: What things are most important to you right now?

We're reminded in James that our time in this life is short and sweet: "What is your life? You are a mist that appears for a little while and then vanishes" (4:14). Every day is a gift from God, so we must always ask ourselves whether it's wise to invest our time in the latest demand. You'll have dozens of opportunities, and therefore decisions, every day. Just because opportunities present themselves doesn't mean you should accept every one of them. It's not realistic, and it's also not wise. Often instead of asking, "Is this right or wrong?" or "Will I enjoy this or not?" we need to ask, "Is this wise in light of my desire to stay grounded in what matters most to me and to God?"

How do you stay grounded in the present by scheduling wisely? You must have the courage to say no. You have to start saying no to good things so you'll be able to say yes to the best things. Too many good things quickly become the enemy of the best things. God calls us to think about time differently from the way most people regard it. We can stay engaged in today, aware of what's most important, or we can lose the present moment like water through our hands. Don't think like everyone else. Don't be afraid to be weird for being wise.

FINDING TIME

People tell me all the time, "Craig, your family is so weird!" Compliment received. Seriously. I find so much comfort in that. The closer our family is to God, the more we stand out from the culture around us. When I'm focusing on what's important to God, I live differently. I invest my time differently. We're happy to be weird. Normal isn't working.

But being weird isn't easy. Just like that night at the restaurant when I realized the family bowing their heads wasn't in prayer, I recently wondered why my house was so quiet (with six kids, silence is usually a signal that something's terribly wrong). Then it dawned on me: every single one of us was immersed in technology. One person was on Facebook, one was working on her blog, one was sending Tweets, one was playing Club Penguin and Webkinz, two were playing Wii (at least they were together), one was listening to her iPod, and one was watching television (yes, my family really is the size of a small village).

That was the day we decided to become weird. Amy and I together made a decision that was very controversial in our home. We limited the use of technology to only three days a week. This means that four days a week there's no television, no iPod, no Facebook, no digital animals you have to feed (even if they'll supposedly starve).

After we unveiled our plan, our youngest son, Bookie, called an emergency conference. All the kids holed up together for more than an hour in a bedroom. Like a platoon leader plotting to storm the enemy line, Bookie led them through his detailed plan for a rebellion guaranteed to overthrow our evil regime.

While learning to sleep with one eye open, Amy and I stuck to our guns, and amazing things started to happen. As we each gradually detoxed from our digital addictions, suddenly we rediscovered board games — Monopoly, Sorry, even checkers. We played charades, told stories, and (gasp!) read books. I've played more matching card games than you could count with my six-year-old, and honestly she beats me every time! Now we have epic wrestling matches that rival anything Wii has to offer, free-for-alls that include all six children spilling from room to room and out into the yard. We have favorite characters (David Copperfield, Anne of Green Gables, Captain Underpants), memorable moments that become the standard for the all-time funniest thing that ever happened, and a lot of laughter. We listen to each other.

What we have now is real. It's genuine. It's truly intimate time that we never had before as a family. And what made it possible was that we were willing to say no to the things to which everyone else says yes. We are far from perfect but willing to be different. We're weird … and blissfully happy together.

If the average American watches twenty-eight hours of TV a week, then by the time she's in her midseventies, she's spent more than *ten years* staring at an electronic box. Is this really how you want to spend your time? Too often the decision to go online, to Facebook, to turn on the TV, to channel surf, to play through one more level of Plants vs. Zombies is made by default. It's an autopilot decision, not a deliberate one. If we are to remain grounded in the present, then we must live deliberately.

LOSING YOUR MARBLES

I read about a dad who realized he was so busy that he was missing most of his kids' lives. He never planned to take them for granted or deliberately chose to miss out on quality time with his kids. But he realized that his time with them would continue to melt faster than a Popsicle in July unless he found a way to slow down and savor the present. So when his oldest daughter was a sophomore in high school, he did something that changed his family's life. The wise father purchased a bunch of marbles.

Back at home, he carefully counted 143 marbles and put them into a large jar. According to the dad's calculation, he had 143 Saturdays left before his oldest daughter graduated high school and left home. So the father put 143 marbles in a jar, and each Saturday he pulled one out. The visual reminded him of the importance of investing his time in the places that mattered. It was inevitable that he would lose his marbles, but at least this way he got to decide where they went.

Interestingly enough for me, my oldest daughter is a little older than his. I've got just over a hundred Saturdays left before she will graduate and leave home. Even as I'm writing this (not helped by the fact that it really is a Saturday morning), I'm tempted to stop immediately and go find her so we can hang out. Maybe it's a compromise, but since I know I'll be with her later today, I'll keep working.

Despite our best efforts, we're all losing our marbles. It's just a matter of how we'll enjoy each one. God gives us an amazing present every day. Normal people leave this gift unwrapped, unrealized, unappreciated, and it's gone before they know it.

Weird people know there's no time like the present.

Chapter 3

THE REST IS
UP TO YOU

*The line dividing work and leisure time is blurring right
before our eyes ... and it's creating a phenomenon called
"weisure time."*

— DALTON CONLEY

R ecently I suffered a relapse in my fourteen-year battle with a
major addiction. No, my setback didn't cost me the pastor-
ate or cause my family to leave me — at least not yet. And
it's probably not what you think. I'm not addicted to drugs or alcohol or
pornography or gambling, but what I battle has the potential to be just as
destructive as any of those. Honestly, it could be even more destructive,
because typically there's no intervention for it.

I'm addicted to adrenaline.

You might wonder how I know I'm addicted to this all-natural drug. Simple: I spent ninety dollars for two one-hour sessions with a trained counseling professional for this diagnosis. Ironically enough, I didn't even want to be there — after all, I didn't think I had a problem. But the leaders of the church where I was serving at the time thought I was dangerously close to workaholic burnout. So to appease them, I went.

At the end of my second session, the counselor gave me an assignment. "This week," he said, peering over his notepad dramatically, "I want you to sit still for five minutes."

And I'm not going to lie to you: I took a good, hard look at the guy and thought, "You've got to be kidding me! This is the worst ninety bucks I've ever spent."

"Five minutes of nonproductivity," he restated. "You can't pray. You can't plan. You can't problem solve. You have to do n-o-t-h-i-n-g."

"Easy," I snapped. "No problem." But deep down inside my productivity-loving heart, I knew it would be a problem. Why sit around wasting time, right? I mean, what in the world could be accomplished by staring out the window for five minutes? Nevertheless, being the compliant — okay, competitive — guy that I am, I was determined to check this assignment off my list like any other appointment. Five minutes of doing nothing — I'd get it done.

It took exactly twenty-eight seconds before I started suffering serious withdrawal symptoms. Lists began unspooling in my mind of all the things I could be doing. All the things that needed doing. All the items that could have been checked off instead of this silly five-minute exercise.

I'm exaggerating slightly, but not by much. The reality is, I couldn't do it. I could not sit still for five minutes straight without doing something.

Seriously, I *could not* sit still and do nothing for five minutes.

(If you're snickering to yourself, thinking, "What a piece of cake," then you should try it. It's harder than you think.)

So I did what any hardheaded, slightly rebellious, type A workaholic would do … I blew off the weird exercise and returned to answering emails that had come in during the one minute and thirty-eight seconds that I had wasted on such silliness and told myself that I didn't really have a problem. With newfound vigor, I returned to my normal life of producing, all the while neglecting the people and true priorities in my life.

I don't have a problem. Do you?

HEALTHY ADDICTIONS

So I obviously flunked the counselor's five-minute "sit still and do nothing" test. A week later I found myself sitting across from him, imagining that I was handing him $1.50 for every minute that passed by — which I was — a thought that made me want to lose my lunch on his expensive carpet.

"Since you're a pastor, would you consider yourself a person who has faith?" he asked me in his most condescending counselor tone.

"Of course," I said in my most pedantic pastor tone.

"I'm sure that's true," my new expensive friend continued, "but when it comes to your schedule, I'm guessing you really don't have much faith."

Where is he going with this?

As he continued, now in a much more soothing and compassionate tone, he started to make sense. "The biggest reason why many people surrender to the normal overwhelmed, overly driven, unsustainable pace," he said slowly for effect, "is because we don't have faith. We don't honestly believe that God is on his throne, that he can and will

We're afraid that if we don't just run nonstop and try everything this world has to offer, we're going to miss out on something.

handle the details of our lives, that he wants what's truly best for us, and that his way of doing life is better."

What a weird way of looking at things ... but could this be true?

"We're afraid," my counselor continued, "that if we don't just run nonstop and try everything this world has to offer, we're going to miss out on something. We're afraid that we might miss that one thing that turns out to be the one elusive piece of our puzzle that will finally fill the void we feel so deeply. But nothing can. There's no such thing as a healthy addiction."

> **I'd elevated my busyness to become an idol that endowed me with a keen sense of self-importance and entitlement.**

Busted — he was dead-on. This was exactly what I'd been doing. I'd been filling my life with things — more of those good (but not best) things that we looked at in the last chapter. I'd elevated my busyness to become an idol that endowed me with a keen sense of self-importance and entitlement. Just because I was addicted to God's work did not mean my fixation was healthy. As Tim Keller explains so well in his great book *Counterfeit Gods*, "Idolatry is not just a failure to obey God, it is a setting of the whole heart on something besides God."[2]

We distract ourselves with "being productive," which makes us look just like everyone else in the world. Our self-worth gets sucked into a riptide of bigger-better-best until we don't know how to break the cycle.

> "A bigger house will make my spouse happy, so that will help my marriage."
> "A nicer car will improve my self-image."
> "Getting a promotion will enhance my lifestyle."

"A lot of 'important people' are going to be at that meeting, so I
     need to be there too."
"I need my body to be as perfect as possible so people will notice
     me and think I'm attractive."
"I have to give my kids everything I never had, and I have to
     make sure they never miss an opportunity."

Sick, destructive, harmful — but normal.

Do you think your spouse would be happy if you lavished time and
attention on him or her instead of being too busy to truly connect? What
if — instead of the new expensive car that put you deeper in debt, causing
you to push it more to make money — you had a reliable car, one that was
completely paid for? What would that do for you? What if you got to do
work that you loved, that was important and used your gifts, and God
met your financial needs through it? What if you had deep and meaningful relationships with virtually everyone in your life, people you knew
you could always count on, and they could always count on you?

Isn't your spirit more important than your body? What if instead of
trying to impress the other members at the gym, you looked after your
health *so you'll be there for your family*? What if your kids learned the
value of a dollar and the fulfillment of working for the things they want
instead of living with the normal sense of entitlement so common today?

You're trying to substitute something for God, when he's the only one who can fulfill you.

What if you invested as much time and energy
into cultivating your kids' spiritual lives as
you did in their vicariously fulfilling your
dream of being a starting pitcher in the major
leagues?

If you feel like you have to produce more
and more and more to fill that vacuum inside

you, make no mistake: it's idolatry. You're trying to substitute something for God, when he's the only one who can fulfill you. This empty pursuit was exactly what I'd been doing for the majority of my life. I was wondering where my time was going instead of wondering where I was going in pursuit of God.

And my counselor's prescription — as weird as it still might seem — is exactly what so many of us need today in order to be restored. We need rest. Strangely enough, often the antidote to idolatry is taking a Sabbath.

COME-TO-JESUS MEETING

If you're addicted to busyness, to the physical thrill of an adrenaline rush because everything depends on your getting today's to-do list completed, then it's time for a come-to-Jesus meeting — literally. In Matthew 11:28 – 30, Jesus says, "Come to me, all you who are weary and burdened, and I will give you rest. Take my yoke upon you and learn from me, for I am gentle and humble in heart, and you will find rest for your souls. For my yoke is easy and my burden is light."

When is the last time you were completely at rest?

Think about this. Jesus doesn't say he'll need you to work overtime, answer every email within twenty-four hours, or keep your home looking like Martha Stewart's. Jesus says he will give you *rest for your souls*: deep, internal rest and peace.

Not asleep

When is the last time you were completely at rest?

If you're like a lot of people, you may not even be sure what it feels like to be completely at rest. Experiencing real rest doesn't mean that you become lazy and unproductive. Take Jesus, for example. He was busy but never hurried. He was productive but never overwhelmed. He accomplished everything God wanted him to do and still spent long, refreshing days in fellowship alone with his Father. Knowing when and how to rest is knowing when and how to acknowledge your limitations and your dependence on God.

Too many of us live constantly with an ever-worsening sickness in our souls. This is the norm today — how you get ahead, how you know you're somebody, how you know you've arrived: by being exhausted on every level and stressed beyond imagination. Mounting pressures at work. Chores at home. Overdue projects. Kids' activities. Grocery shopping. Repairs and maintenance. Commitments. Stress.

Consider how weird it seems for someone to be calm, relaxed, at ease, and peaceful — we usually think such people are either on medication or need to be. Such weirdness dawned on me several years ago when my family was on vacation in the Rocky Mountains. On the drive from Oklahoma to Colorado, I was in my typical rushed-gotta-get-there mode. Timing myself on the highway (racing against who knows what), I strategically limited how much the kids could drink on stops to prevent bathroom breaks every eight miles. (With six kids, wouldn't you do the same thing?)

Once we arrived in Colorado, I felt pressure to make a plan. What would we do? How would we see it all? Which day would we do what? What's the best plan to maximize the trip? How will we know if we had a good time?

On day three, I decided to try my counselor's annoying five-minute assignment that I'd failed before. Sitting on the balcony of our friend's condo, I paused to notice the mountain view along the horizon. Purple, orange, yellow sunlight reflected off the peaks. Red and blue wildflowers bobbing in the breeze of the grassy woodlands at the base of the Rockies. *Wow! Nice work, God.* Before long I started to disconnect. My soul felt like it was thawing. My mind became quieter than I could remember in a long time. I could feel my heart rate start to slow and my breathing become deeper.

Something was happening in my body. My senses seemed to heighten. I could feel the crisp mountain air as I noticed the smell of the distant pines. I saw an eagle soaring effortlessly in the distance. The white clouds seemed to be painted across the deep-blue sky. Without realizing it, I punched off the internal time clock. Five minutes turned to ten, and ten to twenty. My body relaxed as I came down from the adrenaline surge I'd grown accustomed to living on. This process took the rest of the day, as I seemed to unwind and unplug from all the stress that had held me hostage.

The next day, the cool morning air made me feel more alive than I'd felt in months. The snowcapped mountains contrasting with the endless sky seemed like too much to take in. Rather than feeling rushed, I was at peace. Whose schedule were we on, anyway? Isn't that what a vacation is — doing what you want to do when you feel like doing it? Instead of overwhelming me, the noise of my six kids brought me a deep sense of joy. Rather than worrying about work, schedules, and deadlines, I felt at peace with God. He was in control. The world at large would not crumble because I turned off my iPhone.

This is how it's supposed to be.

For the first time in who knows how long, I felt like myself. Fully alive. Fully present. And fully aware of God's goodness.

REST STOP

Let's look again at Jesus' words in Matthew 11:28 – 30: "Come to me, all you who are weary and burdened, and I will give you rest. Take my yoke upon you and learn from me, for I am gentle and humble in heart, and you will find rest for your souls. For my yoke is easy and my burden is light." Maybe you're overwhelmed.

Wouldn't you like rest for your soul? What if rest is not a luxury but a necessity?

Maybe you're hurting. Maybe you're a single parent and you don't think you can make it another day. Maybe your business has collapsed and you're stretched. Jesus is calling you to him. Wouldn't you like rest for your soul? What if rest is not a luxury but a necessity?

As we discussed previously, when you get really busy, there's not enough time to get everything done. You certainly can't take a day off to rest! It's not unusual for people to work six or even seven days a week. Even if their regular job is only five days a week, many people have another part-time job to make ends meet. If they don't, their "days off" are often spent catching up on chores, emails, or errands.

We work harder to accumulate more stuff. Taking care of our stuff consumes more of our time. Pretty soon there's no time left for doing nothing, for relaxing, resting, and being fully present. Not too many years ago, many businesses were not open on Saturday, and none were open on Sundays. Now not only is almost every retailer open seven days a week, but also many are open twenty-four hours a day.

God worked for six days, and as you probably know, on the seventh day he rested. Right off the bat, first things first, the God of the universe, busy creating the earth, the sky, animals, plants, fish, man and woman, and everything else, sets an incredible precedent by setting aside time to rest. This was such a good idea that it led to one of the Ten Commandments: "Six days you shall labor and do all your work, but the seventh day is a Sabbath to the LORD your God. On it you shall not do any work" (Exod. 20:9 – 10).

In Leviticus 25:2 – 4, God told Moses, "The land itself must observe a Sabbath to the LORD. For six years sow your fields, and for six years prune your vineyards and gather their crops. But in the seventh year the land is to have a Sabbath of rest, a Sabbath to the LORD." He told Moses they couldn't sow during that year. "The land is to have a year of rest" (v. 5).

Have you ever heard of a company that would take a year off every

six years? No way! That's crazy! We have to make money! We have to produce! We can't miss all those opportunities! Many business owners (and
customers) think it's weird enough when a Christian-owned company like
Chick-fil-A closes on Sundays. Yet they remain one of the most profitable
fast-food corporations, as well as one of the most respected, in the world.

Their corporate leaders understand this basic principle that God first
gave to the Israelites. By letting the land lie fallow, they allowed depleted
nutrients to restore themselves. This even seemed weird to the Israelites,
since they didn't have county extension agents to perform agricultural
soil testing. God revealed the right thing for them to do, asking them to
trust him on faith. (Today farmers usually rotate crops that draw out different nutrients — and utilize chemical restoration — so they never have
to let the land sit fallow.)

We don't even know how to rest anymore. Most of us take vacations
packed with traveling, activities, and money worries. Then we come back
from our vacation needing a vacation. I took a staycation last year — you
know, when you take your vacation time from work but stay at home. So
I took a few days off to spend with my family. On the first day, I woke up
early, my mind racing with important church matters. I quietly slipped
into my home office and shifted easily into work mode. At about 8:30,
Bookie, my seven-year-old coup plotter, found me at my desk as if he
knew what had to be done if this staycation thing was going to work. He
ran in, flexed his muscles, pointed at me, and called me out: "Dad, I'm
gonna whip you! Let's wrestle!"

More of the Busy Parent's Creed: "I can't yet, buddy. I'll come out in
a few minutes. Daddy's doing something important right now."

Even as the words left my lips, God seared my heart. "*Bookie* is what's
important. Your *work* is the distraction. Close your computer. Don't miss
this moment."

Most of us think we're too busy or too important to rest for a day.

"Do you have any idea how important I am? I can't just let things go!" When you say this (even if not aloud but in your heart), what you're saying is that God's principles are not true. You don't believe God. You don't believe he knows what's best for you: that rest will make you more productive and more spiritually healthy. You need some faith. And you probably need to take a nap.

SUNDAY SCHOOLED

In today's world, for many people, Sunday is just a normal day — another day at work, another day of the weekend for chores and errands, a day to sleep until noon and watch football. Or it could be the busiest day of the week because you and your family spend it going to and coming from church. Although I hope worshiping at church is a life-giving part of your week, I know that it can also be very time and energy consuming (especially for parents). But just as your body

Extreme measures bring extreme results.

needs sleep, your soul needs time to rest in God. To learn more about him. To talk to him. To worship and praise him. To fellowship with other brothers and sisters.

Remember *Chariots of Fire*, the powerful movie about legendary British athlete and Christian missionary Eric Liddell? When Liddell, Britain's Olympic star sprinter at the 1924 Olympics, found out that the first 100-meter race was on Sunday, he decided immediately that he could not run the race. Sunday is God's day, and he was committed to honoring it. Just because he was in Paris to compete in the Olympics didn't justify changing his lifelong commitment.

Most normal people today would think him more than just weird — they would think him foolish for passing up a chance at personal glory and international acclaim. Many in Liddell's country called him a traitor for his bold and unusual stand. Even the Prince of Wales begged him to change his mind. But this uncommon man made an uncommon stand. In the next race, the 400 meters (not run on a Sunday), Liddell beat the runner-up by an amazing fifteen meters! He won the Olympic gold and set a new world record. Though he could have done almost anything with his life after this success, Eric and his family moved back to China to serve as missionaries. Though many would scoff and dismiss his decision as weird, I suspect God would applaud louder than anyone who saw him win the gold medal.

What if you made Sunday worship a nonnegotiable and stuck to it as stubbornly as Eric Liddell did? Or if not Sunday, then one particular, consistent day that's designated to focus on your relationship with God (and with others) and nothing else? What if you decided that if you are in town and not sick, you'd join other believers to corporately worship God? Sound a bit extreme?

Extreme measures bring extreme results.

If you want a normal life, do what normal people do. If you want to know God intimately, walk with him daily, and please him in every way, you're going to have to do what few do.

Absolutely *nothing*.

If you're addicted to your schedule and accomplishments, it's time to do something drastic to break out. If your iPad is your iDol, it's time to put it down. To be fully alive, you need time with God to recharge. Get weird. Normal is not working. You need to rest. You need deep rest. If you are like normal people, you can't keep up this pace. It's time to make a change.

Don't settle for a normal life. Not when you can enjoy the wonderful weirdness of being who God created you to be.

Part Two

MONEY

Chapter 4

RICH
RELATIVES

We are rich only through what we give, and poor only through what we refuse.

— Ralph Waldo Emerson

When you were growing up, who was the richest person you knew? When I was little, the boy who set the gold standard for defining what it meant to be rich was a fabulously wealthy little kid named Richie Rich, star of his own comic book and Saturday morning cartoon. I don't remember how he got his money (oil and gas? dot-com? weekly allowance?), but I do remember he had a butler and a robot maid — which still sounds pretty cool, if you ask me.

How about today — who embodies for you now what it means to be rich? Most of us know someone we consider to be rich: the successful entrepreneur, the hedge fund tycoon, the girl you went to high school with who wrote the bestseller that got made into a big movie starring Jennifer Aniston, who's also rich. If you're like me, chances are that at some point you've thought, "If I were rich like them, I'd be a better rich person than they are. They spend their money on stupid stuff. I'd never do that. I'd only spend my money on good stuff, the right things, ways to help other people."

Problem is, there's someone reading this book right now who's thinking the same thing about you! They would consider *you* rich and think that they would do a better job spending your money than you do. (And they might be right.) Being rich not only involves having rich relatives who leave you a bundle. Being rich is always relative to a shifting standard. When I was young, I believed that if you worked hard, you could make enough money to be considered at least regular rich. If you worked hard *and* had some lucky breaks along the way, then maybe you'd become really rich. And if you worked hard, fell into some great luck, and were beautiful or good-looking enough to marry a gazillionaire, you might even make it to mega-mucho "buy whatever you want and never worry about it" rich. No matter where you rank on the scale, though, chances are that if you're like most people, you'd rather be on the next level higher. Normally, we're never satisfied.

Have you noticed that many rich people don't seem to believe they're rich? I have some wealthy friends. If I took you over to their house to meet them, you'd say, "Yeah, they're loaded." (Then I could take you to their other two homes, and you'd think, "They are *really* loaded.") But whenever someone tells them they're rich, they say, "Oh no, we're not rich. We know these other people who — now, *they're* rich." My friends don't think they're rich, because they know someone who's richer.

The University of Warwick in the UK recently completed a study they called "Money and Happiness: *Rank* of Income, Not Income, Affects

Life Satisfaction" (emphasis mine). As the study's title suggests, their research concluded that for most people, to feel happy about how much money they have, it has to be *more* than what their friends and colleagues have. This turned out to be true no matter how much money someone makes. As long as they know someone who earns more, they aren't satisfied that they are really well off. What they have isn't enough, no matter how much it is.

COMPARATIVE WEALTH

Honestly, these results didn't surprise me. The writer of Ecclesiastes observes, "Whoever loves money never has money enough; whoever loves wealth is never satisfied with his income" (5:10). Talk about timeless — this statement about sums up the normal mindset of people in our culture today. Whatever we have isn't enough. There's always more to earn, spend, buy, shop for, save for, luxuriate in, and go into debt for. The only way to know you're rich is if you can't find anyone who can count higher.

This comparative standard of wealth is further complicated by the fact that the vast majority of us don't consider ourselves anywhere near being rich. If someone asked me, "Craig, are you wealthy?" I'd say, "Are you kidding? I'm a pastor! God provides, of course, but we're far from loaded." My response would be normal. Roughly 98 percent of Americans consider themselves not rich. (And roughly 98 percent of people in developing countries would consider America's poor to be rich.)

Most of us tend to lump ourselves into this not-rich category, even though we've all seen people who are, without question, living on much less than we have. And certainly, there are also people who are certifiably rich whether they choose to believe it or not. We've all seen millionaires and we've all encountered homeless people on city streets, and most of us would identify ourselves somewhere in between. Because cultural and individual standards of wealth are relative, the definition of *rich* always dangles out in front of us. No one seems to know where the true starting line for being rich is located.

Why is that true? It's because rich is a moving target. How you defined rich years ago may not be your standard today. My personal notion of wealth has evolved with each new life season. For example, when I was making twenty-four thousand dollars a year as a pastor, I had a friend who was making forty thousand dollars a year. I distinctly remember telling Amy, "If we could ever make forty thousand dollars a year, we'd never need more than that as long as we live. We'd be rich." Then, of course, we had a child. Then we liked that one so much, we had five more. Rich moved — and left no forwarding address.

The Gallup organization recently polled North Americans, asking them how much annual income they'd need to consider themselves rich. People making thirty thousand dollars a year or less answered (on average) seventy-four thousand dollars a year. People making around fifty thousand dollars a year told Gallup they'd need one hundred thousand dollars a year to be rich. Virtually no one responded in a way that indicated their present annual income as the benchmark for being rich.

Ah yes, the six-figure mark — surely that's an accurate indicator of being rich, right? Viewed objectively as a rich-threshold-crossing number, one hundred thousand dollars certainly makes sense. However, some of you reading this right now are already qualifying such a definition. Is that gross or net? Before or after taxes? With or without insurance? And mortgage payment? And car payments? And — you get the picture. Couples with a combined income of one hundred thousand dollars a year might say, "I've got news for you: That's not rich. With property taxes and a mortgage and kids in college and braces and soccer camp and car insurance, and breast implants for my wife, one hundred thousand dollars a year doesn't go very far."

Another study asked top income earners in the United States how much they'd need to have in assets to *feel* rich. The most common response? A cool five million. If you asked someone with "only" two million dollars, "Are you rich?" she'd say, "Are you kidding? No, I'm not rich." Rich is a moving target. Which explains why normal Americans — even though we're far better off than most people in the world — don't *feel* rich. Therefore we're never satisfied, always wanting more and never appreciating all that we've been given. Once again, being normal is killing us.

LIVING LIKE THE OTHER HALF

Calling what I'm about to tell you good news doesn't do it justice. It's better than good news; it's unbelievably great news! Ready? Maybe you should sit down. Here goes: the good news is, you really are rich![3] Yes, I'm talking to you — no one's reading over your shoulder. And before you roll your eyes and think, "Oh boy, here we go with a pastoral 'you're so much richer than starving people in undeveloped countries' guilt trip," let me stop you. I'm not here to guilt you into giving an extra twenty bucks to the local food pantry or foreign missions team (although I think both are good causes and could definitely use a few more twenties). Or to make you feel bad because you're all warm and cozy (or cool and breezy, depending on where you live) in your nice house with lots of nutritious food in the cupboard and a forty-two-inch flat-screen on the wall. No, my good news for you is that you have opportunities other people don't have — you're rich because you have rich-people opportunities.

You can provide amazing opportunities for your kids to learn, to grow, and to enjoy life. You can have birthday parties for them, take them out to eat, and put them in sports or music lessons. You have reliable transportation that you control. You might be rich enough that you willingly pay so your kids can go to a particular school for an extraordinary education. You might even take your family on annual vacations to places like the beach, the mountains, museums, and heck — even Disneyland. Yep, you're rich. And because God has entrusted you with such riches, you can use these resources to make a profound difference in countless lives. This is very, very good news. Even better than winning the lottery.

More good news is that if you have work that you actually like and you're enjoying blessings in this life, both of those things are gifts directly from God. We're told, "When God gives any man wealth and possessions, and enables him to enjoy them, to accept his lot and be happy in his work — this is a gift of God" (Eccl. 5:19). This verse makes it so obvious. God has blessed you. You're doubly rich.

Now, I realize that you may not be feeling particularly rich at the moment. Our relationship with money is tied to our life circumstances. How we feel about relative wealth is contextual at any given time. You might be hurting financially after enduring a nasty divorce. As if having your heart ripped out and trampled weren't enough, it also left you in a financial mess. You may have fought a major illness and survived its challenges, only to find yourself now facing a mountain of bills so high, you can't see the future beyond them. You might be a single parent with a low-paying job, a deadbeat ex, a bad credit rating, and a car you've raised to life six times. I know a lot of people who are going through circumstances just like these, and they'd say, "You know, I sure don't *feel* rich." Fair enough.

I also know plenty of people in these same situations who complain about what they can't afford, even as they're watching cable on their hi-def TV and eating piping-hot pizza just delivered to their front door, ordered on their iPhone — the one with the unlimited texting and data plan. If we're honest, most of us are doing okay.

LIVING LARGE

Since normal people don't believe they're rich, they generally skim through or skip past anything the Bible says to wealthy people. If you come across a Bible passage that's directly aimed at the rich, how do you respond? From my experience, most of us would say, "Yes, absolutely — those rich people really need to hear God's Word. I'll sure remember this verse if I ever become rich." However, we must remember: God's timeless Word is for the whole planet. When we compare ourselves with the rest of the world, we have to acknowledge that he's talking to us today — we are those rich people!

Visiting a small settlement in a developing country last year, I was struck by the way one of the villagers shared his knowledge of the world beyond his homeland. Since more than half the world lives on less money than most Americans pay for cable TV, you can only imagine how they might describe us. Many would likely say, "There are some people who are so rich, they own a car! It's not a lot of people, of course. I read it's only 3 to 5 percent of people in the world who own a car. But some people in the world are so rich, they have *two* cars! Some of these people even have a *house* for their cars! It's called a garage, and it's like a little house to protect their cars from the elements! You know what else they do? These rich people, they get in their cars, and they drive past twenty or more food places — they call them restaurants — and they're so rich that they pay other people to make their food and serve it to them! That's how rich they are.

"Some of these rich people eat so much food in so many restaurants that they get fat but keep eating more and more. Then they have to go to these places called gyms, and they pay people to help them exercise! That's how rich they are.

"Some of these rich people have special rooms at home called closets.

This little room inside their house is just for their clothes! Nobody sleeps in there — only clothes on hangers and shelves like in a store. Some people are so rich, they even have one big clothes room for the man and one for the woman. So many clothes — some for hot, some for cold, some for work, and some for church. It's crazy! That's how rich people live. I've never seen that with my own eyes. No, no, no. But I've heard about it."

Okay, so my new friend didn't go on and on, but I couldn't help but see our culture through his eyes. In fact, since approximately 50 percent of the world's population lives on less than two dollars a day, any one of nearly three billion people could've easily said everything you just read.

Rich is relative, and we lose sight of how wealthy we really are when we focus only on what we see on TV, in movies, and in magazines. So why don't we feel rich?

ALL CONSUMING

So we're rich but we don't feel rich — how is this possible? It's all because of M&Ms — mass media and mass marketing. Some advertisers want us to feel rich if we can afford their products — they're often called luxury brands and include Mercedes automobiles, Cartier jewelry, and Ralph Lauren clothing. Other marketers want us to feel proud of how cost conscious and value minded we are as smart shoppers. They want us to view their products not as a luxury but as the best quality for the lowest price — think Walmart, Hyundai, and Old Navy.

In either case, we're still encouraged to buy, spend, and shop some more. That's what normal people do. Sadly, such a mindset does not honor God. If you're a follower of Jesus, he has given you abundance so that you can care for others, not so you can stock up on capri pants for next summer or afford a leather interior in the new SUV. As long as you don't own the responsibility of being blessed with resources so that you can give to those around you, then you can stay focused on getting more for yourself. But God's Word and the example Jesus set for us make it Waterford-crystal clear: it's not about us. We find our lives when we give them away. As long as we live in pursuit of more stuff — the latest iToy or coolest shoes — or rely on status symbols to define us (despite the name, a new pair of True Religion jeans won't get us any closer to God), we will never live in true abundance.

We must go from the normal mindset about money and wealth to a radically weird view: gratitude for all we have and stewardship of its use for the good of all. This shift requires us to break out of our usual consumer framework and place ourselves within a global perspective. If you earn thirty-seven thousand dollars a year, you are in the top 4 percent of all wage earners alive today — certifiably rich by anyone's definition. If you make forty-five thousand dollars a year or more, you are in the top 1 percent of wage earners in the world. In order to honor God with your wealth, you first have to admit that you are rich. Most people won't do that. It's not normal.

TRUE PROSPERITY

Just because I'm pointing out how rich we are and how we're supposed to live accordingly, I hope you don't think I'm teaching what's known as the prosperity gospel. This set of beliefs is based on the idea that God wants us to be wealthy and successful (as evidenced by our bank account and possessions), and all we have to do is follow certain biblical principles to make it happen. If you do X for God, he'll give you Y in return. When people ask me how I regard the prosperity gospel, my response is always the same. God blesses each of us with a variety of gifts. He's already prospered us! The real issue is how do we honor him with what we've been given? Maybe I'm so passionate about this topic because ever since I was a kid, I've struggled with the fear that there's not going to be enough. Not enough time in the day (see prior chapters), not enough milk in the fridge, not enough toilet paper in the bathroom, and not enough money in the bank. This mindset has been ingrained in me most of my life, and it absolutely affects the way I think. Foremost, this fear has shaped how I handle money. We've always lived beneath our means; weird as it may seem, we never finance anything. We save for the items we want to buy, and we set aside savings for unexpected expenses.

I always secretly prided myself on how frugal and responsible I was with money. Several people over the years have asked, "Craig, how did you get so good at managing finances? How are you so disciplined about saving money?" They view it as a superhuman feat of self-discipline and brilliant planning — it's good to stay out of debt and save for a rainy day, right? Then one day I realized that my motivation was totally fear-based, not God-honoring. Even though I was handling money responsibly, I was still putting my security in my own abilities to earn and control money so that I would never have to go without anything again. My hope was in material wealth rather than in God's rich provision.

At this realization, I was reminded of 1 Timothy 6:17 – 19: "Command those who are rich in this present world not to be arrogant nor to put their hope in wealth, which is so uncertain, but to put their hope in God, who richly provides us with everything for our enjoyment. Command them to do good, to be rich in good deeds, and to be generous and willing to share. In this way they will lay up treasure for themselves as a firm foundation for the coming age, so that they may take hold of the life that is truly life."

WHAT'S IN *YOUR* WALLET?

My point is that even if we think we're handling money in a biblical way, our real motive may not be pleasing to God. He wants our hearts focused on him, not on imagining every worst-case financial scenario and saving accordingly. Until we identify and face our hearts' attitude toward money, we'll never be able to acknowledge our riches. And until we can realize how rich we truly are, we'll continue to struggle with sharing, giving, and serving others with our resources.

So maybe the question is not "What's in *your* wallet?" but "What's in your *heart*?"

This is basically the question Jesus posed to the Richie Rich of his day. This very wealthy young man came to him and asked how he could be closer to God. Jesus essentially said, "You're going to have to let go of your stuff if you want to be different, if you want to follow me."

The guy said, "I can't do that — I love my stuff too much!" (I'm paraphrasing a little.)

This scene emerges from Luke 18:18 – 30: "Jesus looked at him and said, 'How hard it is for the rich to enter the kingdom of God! Indeed, it is easier for a camel to go through the eye of a needle than for a rich man to enter the kingdom of God'" (vv. 24 – 25). Now, I wasn't a physics major in college, but I know how big a camel is. And I know how tiny the eye of a needle is. Jesus said it's harder for us — the rich people — to enter God's kingdom than it is for a camel to go through the eye of a needle. You don't need to know the original Greek to understand that he means it's hard. *Really* hard.

Why in the world would Jesus say that rich people have an extra-difficult time entering God's kingdom? Was he just like everyone else who resents the rich for having more than him? I don't think so. Instead I believe he's simply making an observation, not a judgment. It's not that a camel's bad behavior prevents it from sliding through that hole in a needle. No, the animal's physical size prevents it.

So maybe the question is not "What's in *your* wallet?" but "What's in your *heart*?"

Similarly, the more a person is able to control life through the power of money, wealth, and status, the more inclined he is to rely on his money's abilities to make things happen, instead of relying on God. It's so hard for us rich people (yes, he's talking to you and me as much as that rich young ruler) to see Jesus, to get him, to believe in him, because honestly we just don't need to rely on him that much. We think our greatest strength is our stuff, our annual salary, our savings account, our credit limit. What if, weirdly enough, our greatest spiritual disadvantage is all this same stuff—possessions, dollars, material items?

Make no mistake: we're rich. And as I see it, being rich brings with it three main challenges.

1. Being Rich Makes It Harder to Depend on God

Most of us in the United States have never had to pray, "Jesus, give me bread today." I know this isn't true of everyone, but it is true of most. Why? Because you've always had a pantry full of bread (or Twinkies or Nacho Cheese Doritos). You've never really known what it's like to trust God to provide for you today, because you've got today provided for. And probably tomorrow too. Maybe even into next winter, with all the food socked away in that extra freezer in the garage.

I know some people who are doing so well at managing their resources that not only are they doing fine not relying on God, but also they've made sure their kids will never have to depend on him either. They have insurance, health care, retirement, and plenty of other safety nets. It's the norm, right? Having these things isn't bad and can be very wise, but they often impede our ability to trust God with our needs.

2. Being Rich Distracts You from True Priorities

Because you're rich, you'll have all sorts of opportunities. You can travel at will. You certainly don't need a church family. You have season football tickets, so you have a valid reason to skip church from September until January. I know people who won't come to church in the summer because they are at their lake house instead. If you are like many, you're rich enough to have your kid in organized sports, and you have to take him to another state because even though he's only nine now, you never know — he might just go pro one day.

You don't really get to pour into your kids because the only time you have together is in the car chauffeuring them between dance, soccer, karate, field hockey, football, gymnastics, glee club, ice skating practice, scuba lessons, and Hooked on Phonics class. And as if all that weren't enough, you have to work harder. Not just to pay all the activity fees and buy all the uniforms but also to keep all the cars and air conditioners and sprinkler systems running. You're distracted with all of your normal rich problems.

If you've never traveled to a third world country, I'd really encourage you to visit sometime (preferably on a mission where you actually get to serve the people who live there). Every time I go, I see people who literally have nothing. I'm talking nothing. Like not even a floor — nothing. Like living on dirt — nothing. Like no indoor toilet — nothing. Like we don't know if we'll be eating today — nothing.

They're different. They're, well … weird. Really weird. "Weirder than anyone I've ever known" weird. So many of these people, all they have is Jesus and each other. It freaks me out every time how full their lives feel despite how little they seem to have that we would consider essential. I find myself strangely jealous of their joy, peace, and simplicity — until I get back home, that is. Then I find myself right back on my iPad, thinking that all the things I've surrounded myself with are key to my happiness.

3. Being Rich Gives You Greater Responsibility

Why do you think God made you rich? Do you honestly believe it was so you could consume it all? A normal response. But Luke 12:48 says,

"From everyone who has been given much, much will be demanded; and from the one who has been entrusted with much, much more will be asked."

Much has been given to us. Because God made us rich, he expects far more from us. How then should we live as rich people?

I'm glad you asked ... It's time for *Lifestyles of the Rich and Weird-for-Jesus.*

Chapter 5

THE BEST MONEY CAN'T BUY

Debt is the worst poverty.

— Thomas Fuller

I just got off the phone with a close friend who is suffocating financially. Seven years ago Jim and his family purchased a comfortably nice three-bedroom home. After they moved in, his wife wanted a new kitchen table and up-to-date wallpaper and drapes, and he wanted — every man's dream — a new gas grill and outside storage unit to house his new riding lawn mower. One thing led to another: new countertops, new carpet, new stainless steel appliances — all compliments of Mastercard and Visa. Reminds me of one of my daughter's favorite stories, *If You Give a Mouse a Cookie*, in which we learn that mice are an awful lot like people when it comes to always wanting more, whether it be more cookies or more nice things. Jim and Beth's lifestyle overflowed with signs of beauty, charm, and good taste: they had a nice house, a nice car, nice clothes, and nice opportunities for their two growing and talented children.

Then one day, unexpectedly, they found out they were expecting.

You might have guessed it. Their new baby added fuel to the new-and-better consumer credit fire that was already burning. Before long it became obvious that their current vehicle and house would be cramped by another child — leading overnight to borrowing for a newer (and larger) SUV and new (and larger) house with four bedrooms instead of three to make sure they had plenty of room for their surprise blessing.

Jim told me painfully, "I don't know what happened. Everything seemed like the right thing to do at the time. We needed a larger house. We wanted a safe vehicle for our baby. And I don't know how we could take our daughter out of dance and cheering or our son out of soccer and baseball. Isn't it normal for parents to want to give their kids the best?"

As I listened to him recount each financial decision he'd made, his story sounded like many others you and I have both heard. Now that he'd lost his job, he was worried he might also lose his house.

Jim looked at me and concluded with hollow resolve, "Well, at least I know that my problems are normal problems."

PRICELESS

You want to know something that's perfectly normal in how we view money? Stress — from not having enough money, not making enough money, and owing way too much money. So many people I know live paycheck to paycheck; with the recent economic struggles we've had, you may be in the same boat. According to a recent survey by CareerBuilder

.com, more than half — 61 percent — of working Americans live paycheck to paycheck.[4]

Monthly payments? Normal. Credit card debt? Normal. Paying only the monthly minimums? Normal. Yes, in fact it's *priceless*. Because what price can you place on your worry, anxiety, and fear? How much are your health, security, and peace of mind worth? Since everyone fights this battle, though, surely it's worth the war — right? It's only normal ... All we want is what we think everyone else has. But everyone else has only the same stress, worry, and despair that we have. And the collateral damage of all this normalcy? Tension in your relationships with the people you love the most. Fights between you and your spouse. Feelings of helplessness and frustration. Powerlessness and despair. Shame and embarrassment. Since it's been at least a few pages since I've brought it up, you know why I'm so against being normal? Normal. Does. Not. Work.

How many of us typically spend more each month than we earn? And how do we cover the gap? Credit cards, depleted savings, payday loans, and early 401(k) withdrawals. What would it be like to have money left over at the end of the month? To pay all your bills and save money? Please don't hear me passing judgment or feeling superior. I shared earlier how my frugality and commitment to living debt free were really just the flip side of this same shiny coin — wanting to feel in control of my life. The problem with keeping the focus on ourselves and spending all or more than we earn is that we miss out on the blessing of giving it away to others. I know, you may be saying, "I don't have enough to get by on myself — how can I worry about giving to anyone else?"

Most people say that the reason they don't give more is that they don't feel they can afford it; they feel they don't have enough. What if you had enough to, say — oh, I don't know — help someone in need? What if you had enough extra money available that you could give some away and not feel stressed about it? What if you had enough money available to do what you enjoy most? What if you even had enough money available that you could exchange some of it for more time in your schedule? (For example, say you could pay someone to clean your house or take care of your yard.) Extra financial oxygen gives you more room to breathe. It can help you feel rested. Not anxious, worried, and always afraid — you know, like normal.

Considering what a destructive distraction money troubles can be, it's not surprising that God wants you free from financial worry. He wants you to have extra. Proverbs 21:20 is a great verse to memorize: "In the house of the wise are stores of choice food and oil, but a foolish man devours all he has." The wise — not the rich — have more than enough in their house. They have extra. According to this verse, it's a foolish person who lives paycheck to paycheck. Every time he gets more, he uses it all up. Don't you think it's weird that the Bible *doesn't* say you have to be wealthy to have more than enough? According to this verse, you don't have to be a two-income family. You don't need six figures annually. You only have to be wise. There's a wise way to manage the money God entrusts to you. And there's a foolish way to (mis)manage what God entrusts to you. The choice is really yours.

RICHER THAN RICH

Some good friends of ours, two different families, have very different homes. I'm guessing both couples are similar to people you know. Mike and his wife, Brenda, live like many of the people in our local community. They have a beautiful, four-thousand-plus-square-foot home. Their yard is manicured, professionally cared for. The massive entryway into their house features double doors opening off a long, beautiful porch. Even their doorbell is awesome. It's not just *ding-dong*. It's DONG-*da-ding-da*-DONG-*dong*!

Walking in, I always feel like I'm entering a hotel; the impression is immediately tasteful, inviting, open, grand. High ceilings, wood floors bordering expensive tile, a prominent curvy staircase. The kitchen shimmers with stainless steel appliances. My wife envies their expansive gas stove (not to mention the water spout perfect for pot-filling right next to it). Granite countertops everywhere.

Every room exudes their expensive good taste — even the bathrooms. Marble vanities and antique-looking fixtures. The toilet is huge and so high up that when you sit on it, your feet dangle like a little kid's (not that mine have). Their garage — if you could call it that — looks more like a giant showroom with shiny cars in it. Lined with storage cabinets, it has four bays. Brenda has a big SUV. Mike has a fully loaded, very classy sedan so he can chauffeur clients around when they're in town. They also have a flashy bright convertible "just for fun." The remaining bay holds their ski boat and the kids' twin Sea-Doos.

Their whole house sends a clear message: Mike and Brenda are enviously successful. They're doing well. Very well. It's so obvious that not only do they have a lot of money, way more than they need, but also they have good taste and cool, insider's knowledge about the best stuff their money can buy.

But Mike let me in on what their successful lifestyle is costing them — much, much more than any dollar amount. You see, they're honestly *not* doing so great. Behind the granite, marble, and hardwood floors, they don't really have any financial means, no margin whatsoever.

Brenda recently had to return to work. She wanted to stay home and take care of their kids and the house, but that's just not a realistic option anymore. Mike's constantly afraid he's going to lose his job. They're in a desperate race, grasping to maintain their lifestyle. Both of them are constantly tired, overextended, and afraid. They snipe and snap at each other more and more, just as the late fees and overdraft charges pile up more and more. I'm convinced they do love each other, but they blame each other for their circumstances, and you can see it in how they vent their frustration (and fear) on each other. Sure, their house has fantastic curb appeal, but you sure wouldn't want to live there. The writer of Proverbs 13:7 could have been describing their home when he said, "One man pretends to be rich, yet has nothing."

Then there's Tony and Erryn. When you walk up to their house, the first thing you notice is their shabby, dandelion-infested yard. Cluttered with toys and footprints, it looks as if every kid in the neighborhood lives there — and they practically do. You can push the doorbell if you like, but it doesn't work. When I knock on the cheap, flimsy screen door, Tony always gives me a hard time about it: "You're family! If it's unlocked" — which it always is — "then come on in!"

The narrow entryway is dimly lit, but the ceilings will take your breath away — that is, provided you're a fan of that seventies-style popcorn texturing. The kitchen is small and sparse but really functional. When you come in, Erryn, quite the cook, grabs you. "Try this! You'll love it," she says, smiling, as she shoves a spoon in your mouth. And she's always right — soup or spaghetti sauce or something fruity — it's delicious, and you instantly want more.

The countertops are genuine Formica, a bit faded and even cracked in a few spots, but great for leaning on or spilling Kool-Aid on or chopping vegetables for Erryn's next creation. Their bathroom has just one sink, one toilet, and one bathtub. But there's something cozy and charming about it. Erryn is an artist, so she's made little towels that read "Welcome," "Love," and "Friends." Although not as small as their bathroom, the garage is seriously *tiny*. They have two cars — both with more than a hundred thousand miles, and one with considerably more than that — but only one car fits in there. Tony's older little-car-that-could stays outside like a devoted pet, shamelessly braving the elements.

I absolutely *love* coming to their house, and I tell them this almost every visit. It feels like, well … home. I kick my shoes off right inside the front door and just hang out in my socks. Their soft couch practically begs me to crash for a nap on it. Maybe it sounds weird (I'm sure you've become accustomed to this from me by now), but it feels like I live there. It's so peaceful. It hums and breathes and whispers to slow down, relax, be yourself. You can feel it everywhere. They have plenty of money, more than they need. Nobody ever goes hungry there, especially not guests.

Tony and Erryn have chosen a simpler lifestyle. When I fall into their old recliner to watch a game with Tony on their smallish thirty-six-inch television and see how they and their kids all interact with each other, they're different. They're not just family; they actually seem to enjoy each other — to want to be around one another and share things together. Crazy, I know — downright weird. They don't have a lot of nice things or photo-shoot-ready rooms staged with new furniture. So they don't really care if something accidentally gets broken. You can't imagine the peace there. Eating a sandwich over their sink is more therapeutic than getting a massage. No tension, fear, and anxiety. No pressure to focus more on their stuff than on them.

The casual observer approaching their house would say, "They are so out of it — did you see all those dog hairs? And the furniture? Not to mention that non-hip retro-original wallpaper. Shame they can't afford better." But they'd be dead wrong. The problem isn't that they can't afford what many would consider better.

The problem is that we've been defining better — rich, successful, cool, acceptable — the wrong way. Mike and Brenda's huge house, with its picture-perfect rooms, reeks with tension, frustration, and fear. It offers nothing to make guests feel secure, relaxed, at ease. No, the whole vibe in that house whispers instead, "This is illusion. A house of cards about to fall."

Tony and Erryn's home, on the other hand, creates a kind of envy that can't be quenched by a trip to Ethan Allen. Their home is rich in love, brimming with margin, with room to make mistakes, and time to just hang out. Their family has what matters most. "In the house of the wise are stores of choice food and oil, but a foolish man devours all he has" (Prov. 21:20). Again, I'm not trying to judge my friends, but I know because of what each couple has shared with me. One works hard to prop up an illusion that sucks the life out of them, and the other works hard to make their home a place that restores them, nurtures them, and gives life to others.

CONTENTMENT FOR DUMMIES

It seems like we can always count on Paul to make things obvious for us. In 1 Timothy 6:6 – 8, he writes, "Godliness with contentment is great gain. For we brought nothing into the world, and we can take nothing out of it. But if we have food and clothing, we will be content with that." Tony and Erryn embody this kind of contentment. They're godly with contentment, holy with their homemaking. Not a little gain. Not just some gain. Not "Aw, shucks, we're just poor, humble people getting by." No, *great* gain! They're deliberately choosing their lifestyle, just as Mike and Brenda chose theirs.

Paul goes on in verses 9 and 10 to describe the painful cycle so many people find themselves in: "People who want to get rich fall into temptation and a trap and into many foolish and harmful desires that plunge men into ruin and destruction. For the love of money is a root of all kinds of evil. Some people, eager for money, have wandered from the faith and pierced themselves with many griefs."

It's the foundation of Temptation 101. It *looks* so good, but it's a trap. Just listen to how serious — downright dangerous — his words are: Trap.

Foolish. Harmful. Plunge. Ruin. Destruction. All kinds of evil. Pierced. Griefs. What are some of the griefs piercing the normal people we know? Debt. Financial pressure. Stress. Tension. And over what? Money? In *Charlie and the Chocolate Factory*, I love what Charlie's grandpa tells him when Charlie wants to sell his golden ticket because their family really needs the money: "There's plenty of money out there. They print more every day. But this ticket, there's only five of them in the whole world, and that's all there's ever going to be. Only a dummy would give this up for something as common as money. Are you a dummy?"

Godliness with contentment is rare. It's weird. All of us know people who can't enjoy the blessings that God has provided to them because they're always worried about money. That's common. And why does it stress them so much? Because they're so desperate to *keep it all*. That's the fear, isn't it? That you'll have to give some up, have to lose some of that great stuff that goes along with it. Maybe the reason why clinging to it all feels so stressful is because we're not supposed to.

There's plenty of money. If you want to be different, if you want to be better than normal, then you must *live* differently. This is the one life that God has given you. According to the gospel of Charlie's grandfather, "Only a dummy would give it up for something as common as money."

THE SECRET TO DEBT-FREE LIVING — IN FOUR EASY PAYMENTS!

If you've ever suffered insomnia and spent the wee hours of the morning channel surfing, you know that many people are getting rich by telling the rest of us how to get out of debt. Or if you've cruised through the bestsellers at your local Barnes & Noble, you can also find an entire section devoted to the secrets of debt-free living. Now, I'm not talking about the legitimate financial experts who have sound principles and inspiring methods of being fiscally responsible. I'm a big Dave Ramsey fan, and there are many other excellent resources that I would endorse wholeheartedly.

Enough is never enough.

My problem with some of the other financial gurus is that they clearly seem to be exploiting our desire for a quick fix. I hate to shout out the obvious here, but none of us dug our debt pit overnight. My friends Jim and Beth, as well as Brenda and Mike, didn't set out to fall head over heels in debt. It was that "one thing leads to another" trap — if you give a mouse a cookie, he wants a glass of milk.

Enough is *never* enough.

Most of us have lifestyled our way right into the black pit of normal. It feels like it's an income problem. Most people think, "If only I made just a little more money! It wouldn't take much. Then I could fix everything going on in my life." But it's not an income problem. It's a lifestyle problem. As your income goes up, your lifestyle trails along and catches up, gobbling up with it any chance you have at extra. At its root, it's actually more than just a lifestyle problem; it's a spiritual problem.

In Matthew 6:19, Jesus says, "Do not store up for yourselves treasures on earth, where moth and rust destroy, and where thieves break in and steal." But most people's lifetime ambition is the exact opposite of that: store and get more. More, more, more. Jesus continues, "Store up for yourselves treasures in heaven, where moth and rust do not destroy, and where thieves do not break in and steal. For where your treasure is, there your heart will be also" (vv. 20 – 21).

Where your money goes, there your heart follows.

The average Christian in the United States gives about 2 percent of his or her income toward helping people and advancing God's kingdom on the earth. That means that the remaining 98 percent goes to the world. Which means that 98 percent of our hearts go toward the world. If you catch yourself wondering why you want more of the world and you're not satisfied with God, it's because you have a spiritual problem. We think that more is going to make us happy.

First John 2:15 – 17 gives us fair warning: "Do not love the world or anything in the world. If anyone loves the world, the love of the Father is not in him. For everything in the world — the cravings of sinful man, the lust of his eyes and the boasting of what he has and does — comes not from the Father but from the world. The world and its desires pass away, but the man who does the will of God lives forever."

If you want to get out of debt forever, the secret is that there's no secret. It's like losing weight — no matter how many fad diets or gimmicks people come up with, there's no quick fix. You have to change the way you eat — less bad stuff and more good stuff — and you have to exercise. Overcoming debt is the same way. It's basic math. Fortunately, it's elementary math, not nuclear physics. The two options on the path to financial margin are simple:

1. Earn more.
2. Spend less.

Where your money goes, there your heart follows.

That's it. The secret to getting out of debt, right there in a nutshell. You knew that, and I trust you also know that I'm not trying to insult your intelligence or express anything other than encouragement about how to get out of the normal money trap that's killing so many people. So if we know the solution, what keeps us from implementing it? There has to be a deeper issue, a root problem. To get rid of a spiritual problem, we need to pull it up by its spiritual root. To pull up roots, we're going to have to be willing to get our hands dirty, to make some sacrifices that provide long-term benefits instead of short-term, refinanced gains. God is willing to help us, to provide the tools we need to weed out those areas where our desire for money is spoiling our fruit of the Spirit.

Proverbs 15:16 says, "Better to have little, with fear for the LORD, than to have great treasure and inner turmoil" (NLT). Better a little with God than a whole lot without him. Better to have fewer houses, cars, appliances, clothes, toys, and bills than to have the whole world and lose your soul. Better something paid for that's used and enjoyed and shared and worn out than something nice and shiny and new that won't be paid for until 2019 and that you're too stressed to enjoy. Better a little with the fear of the Lord than more of what everyone else has. Better than normal, instead of normal is best.

You must long for God more than normal.

The world says more will make you happy. But this is the mirage in the desert of twenty-first-century life — you can never get there. God says happiness is contentment with what you already have, with what he provides you, with what you can share. If you struggle to believe this, then you must pierce the veil of illusion our culture works so hard to sustain. You must long for God more than normal. You must be willing to live to give, not live to gain. It's like Jesus asking the lame man beside the healing waters of Bethesda, "Do you want to get well?" (John 5:6). Obviously, he wasn't insulting this invalid, who was clearly there intent on being healed.

So do *you* want to be well? Do you want to escape from debt? Then you have to make a choice about what matters most and then act on your heart's desire. It's normal to be sick over money in our culture today. In order to be healthy — and experience the joy of eternal riches — it's time to get weird.

Chapter 6

A GENEROUS EYE

We make a living by what we get, but we make a life by what we give.

— WINSTON CHURCHILL

M y kids are weird — maybe even weirder than I am. Sure, they do a lot of regular-kid stuff, but I overhear them sometimes and think, "Normal kids just don't talk about stuff like this." When my two youngest, Jojo and Bookie, were five and six, they once had this heated discussion in the backseat of our car on a family road trip. (You're probably thinking, "No wonder they're weird, with names like Jojo and Bookie." I know. Sometimes nicknames just stick.) I'm not sure how it started, but here's where their conversation ended up:

Bookie: "Joy, you've *got* to give your money to charity. When you give your money to charity, you're giving it to God!"

Jojo: "I'm not giving my money to charity."

Bookie: "Please, Joy! You *have* to give your money to charity. Giving your money to charity is like giving it to God."

Jojo: "I am *not* giving my money to charity."

Bookie: "Please, Jojo — please, please, puh-leeeze ... Give your money to charity, even just some of it, and you'll be giving to God!"

Jojo: "Look, Bookie, I'm not giving anything to Charity — I don't even know who she is! And if I did, I probably wouldn't like her anyway. Charity is not getting any of my money!"

You may be tempted to agree with Jojo. It's not easy to get the things we have; we work hard to maintain the lifestyles we've grown accustomed to having. It's perfectly normal to feel entitled to keep what's ours. Especially if we don't personally know the people to whom we're giving (and if you're like Jojo, even if you do), then it's easy to think, "Let them earn their own! It's every man for himself — there's no way I'm giving my money, my time, my resources to anyone." But Bookie was onto something foundational to understanding our relationship to money and material possessions. The Bible consistently and directly indicates that when we give generously, we're serving, honoring, and glorifying God. After all, generosity is fundamental to God's nature.

If you're a follower of Christ, consider just for a moment the value of the incredible, undeserved gift he has given to us. Mercy. Grace. Forgiveness. A new life. It's hard to fathom just how freely he's lavished us with all that he has. If we've received the heart riches and abundant life of a new life through Christ, we should be giving out of the deepest gratitude. And we should also realize that nothing else really matters if we have what God gives so freely. We can give away all that he entrusts to us in the same spirit of generosity.

EYE ON THE PRIZE

God's Word gives us a simple but awesome promise: "He who has a generous eye will be blessed" (Prov. 22:9 NKJV). I love the way this is worded, "a generous eye." It's simultaneously fresh and timeless, so easy to understand and yet so powerfully true. I know several business leaders with an eye for the best deal. Designers may have an eye for color. You may have an eye for details or for the big picture. But all of us can have a generous eye — it's not a special talent, skill, or personality trait. And all of us can experience the consequence — being blessed — of such a generous attitude. What would you see if you looked at the world through generous eyes? Going through your daily life, you might notice needs that escape other people, or identify places where you alone are capable of giving what's needed. Seeing with generous eyes would color your thinking beyond yourself:

> "God, who can I bless in this present situation?"
> "What do I have that I could use to make a difference?"
> "What is the need here — and what can I do to meet it?"

Weirdly enough, the more we give away, the richer we become. We're promised a blessing when we have a generous eye. But what exactly does this mean? Are we back to the prosperity gospel — giving only so that we can get more in return? No, the blessing we receive in return may not be material at all. Jesus explains this promise another way: "Give, and it will be given to you. A good measure, pressed down, shaken together and running over, will be poured into your lap. For with the measure you use, it will be measured to you" (Luke 6:38). He too indicates that there's a cause-effect, reciprocal relationship between giving what we have and receiving God's blessing. When you give, you will be blessed. When you give, it will be given back to you.

Paul was friends with people who had walked shoulder-to-shoulder with Christ, and he quotes Jesus in Acts 20:35: "It is more blessed to give than to receive." You've probably heard this verse before, but most of us certainly don't think this way. It's counterintuitive. We'd much rather get something than give something away.

I'm not suggesting that when you give a hundred dollars somewhere, you're going to get back a hundred dollars (or more) somewhere else. Certainly, this can happen, but it's not the point. This truth is not an investment strategy for manipulating God like you'd play the stock market. We're promised a blessing if we give generously, not a big payback. Not all the blessings of God have to do with money; instead, they may be riches of the Spirit — peace, joy, patience — or gifts that money can't buy (a spouse, kids, forgiveness, respect, a job you love). In God's economy, you may even harvest a crop in places where you didn't plant seed. When you're generous, you will be blessed, whether it comes to you materially, spiritually, emotionally, relationally, or some other way. God obviously cares much more about what happens in our hearts than what happens in our bank accounts, more about our attitudes than our credit scores. Giving generously changes you. It frees you up, undermines the power that money and possessions can have over you, and it makes you more like him.

RICH IN SPIRIT

A couple of years ago my whole family went on a mission trip to Ecuador. We served in several different villages while we were there and met a variety of native peoples. In one particular town, the residents' appearance reminded us of Native Americans back home in the United States. Although my kids are one-sixteenth Cherokee, one of my daughters, Mandy, looks more like she's fifteen-sixteenths Native American. She blended right in with the townspeople while we were there and looked like she belonged. The villagers were really polite to everyone in our group, but they didn't necessarily connect with us. Mandy, on the other hand, had these sweet people swarming all around her, like she was their long-lost daughter at a family reunion.

As we got acquainted with the people in this village, I started asking some of my usual questions: what's their food source, what kind of jobs do they do, how do they make enough money to live on. I discovered that they have a fairly large trade making beautiful, elaborately embroidered dresses. They take great pride in their lovely work, and many wealthy people from around the world come there to purchase it — often for a special occasion for their daughters or wives. According to the villagers, the average dress takes about a month to make — not hard to believe when I considered the incredible details, colorful decorations, and beautiful tailoring of each one. They explained that one dress usually sells for enough money to support a family's basic needs for one month. And I do mean basic, since this amount only averages out to a meager three dollars a day. It provided enough for food, some clothing, and medicine if needed, but the family remained in profound poverty: no running water, no electricity, dirt floors.

When we finished our service project there, our team began packing up and getting ready to leave. Just as we were about to say goodbye, our translator approached, trailed by a group of people from the village. Through the translator, smiling broadly the whole time, the villagers told us, "We believe God wants to bless your daughter Mandy with one of our dresses."

I didn't know what to say. It just felt so wrong — we were there to serve them, not take a month's wages out of their hands. I tried to thank them graciously even as I made it clear why we couldn't accept such an extravagant gift. They insisted, "No, no, you must. We believe God really wants to bless her."

My mind wandered to all the clothes in Mandy's closet at home, all that we had waiting for us back in our normal lives in the States. We have so much and they have so little; it just didn't seem right. So I offered, "I will pay you for it, but I simply cannot let you just give it to her. No — no way."

My translator started to turn his head toward them but remained fixed on my words. He maintained eye contact with me for several uncomfortable seconds, standing silently, before he finally said, "Pastor Groeschel, I won't tell them this. It would hurt them very badly. Please, it would be very rude for you to rob them of the blessings they would like to give you and your family on behalf of God."

Tormented as I was over the inequity, I knew that accepting their gift, no matter how extravagant, was the right thing to do. As they placed the dress over Mandy's head to try it on her, her tears started to flow. Mine did too. And Amy's. In fact, by the time they had her all laced up, every one of our team was sobbing! Their entire village was just one giant smile. I felt so unworthy, so humbled. How could our family receive such a luxurious gift?

God clearly seemed to be telling our family, "I want to teach you to receive from me. Remember where all blessings come from."

BLESSED TO BE A BLESSING

Why does God bless us? To change us and reshape us and undo the damage we do to ourselves by settling for a normal life. Mandy's dress reminds me still of how arrogant we can become to assume we need nothing from the poor — when many in fact have more substantive wealth than we have. I'm convinced God doesn't bless us because we deserve it or because we earn it. He doesn't bless us to make us feel guilty and ashamed. He blesses us so we can be different.

Paul writes in 2 Corinthians 9:11, "You will be made rich in every way so that you can be generous on every occasion, and through us your generosity will result in thanksgiving to God." Notice that he didn't say "rich in finances." He said "rich in *every way*." The Greek word for "every way" is *pas* (pronounced "pahss"), which means every, any, all, the whole, all things, or everything. Most people — even believers — seem to pursue only material blessings. If this is our only definition of riches, however, we're missing out on 99.9 percent of what else God has to offer. "Every way" includes relational, emotional, psychological, physical, and … well, all the ways you can imagine. Financial and material are certainly included, but they're just two of the dozens of categories of riches.

Why did Paul say God would make us rich in every way? "So that … your generosity will result in thanksgiving to God." God is always concerned with turning people toward himself and toward his purposes — loving other people. Why? *Because he wants us to know him and how much he loves us.*

When you let God's blessings flow through you, and you give generously as his conduit of blessing, then you will radically depart from the typical mindset of "what's in it for me?" Which means most normal people won't get it. They won't understand — why in the world would you give away so much of what you have? But you'll definitely have their attention with your supernatural generosity, and they'll want to know what's different about you. They'll ask you how you can give — and live — so freely. And you'll have an opportunity to explain why you're so weird and why they might want to consider being weird too. Why? It's not just because normal isn't working. More important, it's because God is our only true source of life.

3-D GLASSES

The only way to cultivate a generous eye is to practice — to look for opportunities and then give in to them. I've found it helpful to categorize these opportunities into three ways of giving — looking through the 3-D glasses of generosity, as it were. Practicing all three draws us closer to God, to his way of seeing things, but as we progress through the three dimensions of giving, we grow stronger in our eternal perspective. Suddenly we view the needs of others as more important than our own. We discover that the sticky power of money and possessions doesn't glue us in place like it once did. We discover that we don't get anxious or worried about what we need or what's going to happen.

The first level of giving is spontaneous. Certainly, there's nothing wrong with being a spontaneous giver. When you see a need, you immediately want to pounce on it and fill it. Notice a homeless man at the busy intersection with a sign asking for food money? Then slip him a bill before the light changes. Hear about a family that doesn't have transportation? Then loan them your minivan for a week. All good impulses. However, if spontaneous giving is your only exercise, then it limits the impact you can have — and the impact God's blessing can have on you.

This first-level giving is not a deliberate lifestyle commitment, only a reaction, and often an emotional one at that — compassion for the homeless person, guilt over the unused car in your garage. Again, not a bad thing — but simply not enough to cultivate a consistent generous vision. The goal is to transform spontaneous giving into what I call strategic giving.

If spontaneous givers are weird, then strategic givers are just plain rowdy. Strategic givers plan ahead so they can be really generous. They're intentional. They think it through. Isaiah 32:8 describes this kind of giver: "Generous people plan to do what is generous, and they stand firm in their generosity" (NLT). Strategic givers actually contemplate questions like "How can we be *more* generous? How can we make our eyes generous? How can we maximize the blessings we have so we can be a blessing to others?"

I will give God my first and best, and he will bless the rest. Strategic givers are also tithers. They understand the biblical principle: I will give God my first and best, and he will bless the rest. They acknowledge that the first part of everything they make belongs to God and that they're only returning to him (through his church and his work) what's already his, out of obedience and love.

Many families, including my own, commit to such a strategic approach of giving and tithing. Amy and I schedule a monthly meeting to review: "Where are we giving? Are we seeing impact? How much do we have left to give? How much more do we need to give going forward?" This kind of intentionality has blessed us — and been used by God to bless others, we hope — into becoming stronger, better givers. We don't simply react to our emotions or the overt need under our noses. The strategic giver realizes: giving is not something we do; generous is who we are. True to God's promise, when we commit to giving consistently, we grow closer to him and see his purposes with new eyes.

Finally, to give us the full-on, hi-def, IMAX experience of giving, we have the sacrificial givers. If spontaneous givers are weird and strategic givers are rowdy, then these folks are straight-up, wild-eyed fanatics. They're crazy. They're scary. They don't just believe that the things of this world don't matter; they completely live that way. More than simply acknowledging with their words that material things aren't what it's about, they actually see possessions as merely tools that God provides for us to advance his kingdom on earth.

Sacrificial giving doesn't mean you toss everything to the wind and have nothing. In fact, many sacrificial givers are quite wealthy — they just don't live like it's their goal. They have so much, and know they're merely God's stewards of it, that they delight in sharing it — spontaneously, strategically, and sacrificially. They love and trust God so much that they have no problem with letting go of what he's temporarily given them to take care of.

When you hear regular people in our culture say, "I don't really have enough to give," what they're actually saying is that they don't feel like they have enough *extra*, enough left over, that they can give without adjusting their lifestyle. This is normal, of course. However, the truth is that you always have *something* you can give. And the less you have, the more your sacrifice means. Jesus observed the widow who gave all she had as an offering at the temple and considered it so amazing that he shared its significance with his disciples (Mark 12:41 – 44).

The more we have, the greater the responsibility and opportunity — to be a blessing. "From everyone who has been given much, much will be demanded; and from the one who has been entrusted with much, much more will be asked" (Luke 12:48). The more we cultivate a generous eye, the more clearly we can see — ourselves, others, and God.

But have you ever gotten a headache from wearing 3-D glasses to watch a movie? I'm guessing that you may be feeling the same way now, particularly if you haven't had much practice with giving. I understand and have felt this way before. Don't worry, though. Here's all you have to do: start where you are. If you haven't been giving at all, then start. Give spontaneously. See a need you can meet and meet it.

Giving is not something we do; generous is who we are.

But don't stop there. Start saving. Start cutting back so you'll have more that you can give. Watch for opportunities. Plan, pray, and start giving strategically. Just as you now think about how to get the things you want, consider how to look ahead so you can give in even more dramatic, life-impacting ways.

But don't stop there. Get crazy. Get weird. Be willing to feel it. Press in. Get fanatical. Study your finances. Study your lifestyle. Figure out how to live on less. And less. And less. And give more. And more. And more.

I want to be 100 percent clear here. I'm not trying to talk you into giving as much of your money to your church as you possibly can. That's not God's economy. And frankly, that would be really lazy of you. In fact, don't do that. Give 10 percent — at a minimum — to your local church. Support it. Water where you've been planted. Help that grow. As you gradually increase that percentage over time, look beyond your local church for other places that you can help grow. Meaningful ministries. Opportunities in your neighborhood, in your kids' school. Causes you feel passionately about that can advance God's kingdom. Leverage the resources you have to change eternity. And learn how to save and earn even more resources so you can give even more.

Sure, it's weird to believe that it's more blessed to give than to receive. But it's also the most life-giving, eye-opening truth about money that we can ever learn. Do whatever you have to do to make your eyes generous. God will bless you, and you can be a blessing.

Part Three

RELATIONSHIPS

Chapter 7

LOVE IS ... WEIRD

*We are all a little weird and life's a little weird, and when
we find someone whose weirdness is compatible with ours,
we join up with them and fall in mutual weirdness and
call it love.*

— ATTRIBUTED TO THEODOR GEISEL, "DR. SEUSS"

C raig, you *have* to meet this girl! She's *weird* — like you!"
This was the first description I was given of Amy, the
woman who became my wife over twenty years ago. Back in
college when I heard these words, though, I wondered if such a thing
could be possible — a girl as weird as me? And was this a good-weird and
therefore a kind of backhanded compliment of my own weirdness? Or
more in the *weird*-weird category and this speaker's attempt at putting

me in my place? I mean, hearing that a woman is weird isn't an automatic turn-on for most hormone-fueled twentysomething males. "What do you mean, she's weird — like *me*?" I shot back to Sara, my classmate, who was obviously enjoying the opportunity to make it clear that she herself was not weird and was therefore not my type.

Sara's jabs were not without reason, and she definitely piqued my interest in how we were each defining the W label. "Tell me, what's so weird about this girl?"

"Everything," she replied. "She's just not normal . . . I mean, she's nice and all. You just have to meet her and you'll see. To be honest, she's weird like you — all into the God thing." This sounded promising, but I confess (again, as the twentysomething red-blooded guy I was at the time) that I couldn't imagine that Sara's friend could actually be into God and pretty *and* weird. These things just didn't seem to go together much, from my experience at the time. If a girl was weird . . . well, it was probably because she couldn't attract a normal guy.

Nonetheless, I was excited by the prospect of meeting someone who wasn't trying to live like everyone else. Becoming a Christian had changed the way I saw normal dates with normal girls — primarily because my focus changed from one of physical pleasure to one of spiritual compatibility. So I prayed for two months before calling Amy for the first time, patiently asking God if he really wanted me to reach out to someone I'd only heard about. After lots of praying, I made the call.

If you haven't guessed by now, it wasn't a normal "let's go on a blind date" kind of call. As you read this story, keep in mind that this is 100 percent true, exactly as it happened. Giddy after two months of prayer and anticipation, I called Amy's home number. No cell phones or Facebooking then. (Yes, I'm *that* old.)

Ring. Ring. Ring. Her answering machine picked up: "Hi, this is Amy. I'm not home right now. Please leave a message after the beep."

The beautiful sound of her voice was instantly familiar. *Could she and I really be from the same tribe of weird?* As odd as it sounds, I honestly had a strong sense, sight unseen, that I would marry this girl one day. Since this would be her first impression of me (her future husband), I knew my message had to be memorable.

For context, the Tom Cruise movie *Top Gun* was really popular then. In one memorable scene, Carol (played by Meg Ryan) says to Goose (Cruise's sidekick, played by Anthony Edwards in his pre-*ER* days), "Hey, you big stud, take me to bed or lose me forever!" Inspired to mimic this line in my own spiritualized version, after the beep I said, "Hey, you Christian babe, take me to church or lose me forever!" I then finished my first message to my future wife with a relevant Bible verse: "'And now these three remain: faith, hope and love. But the greatest of these is love.' First Corinthians 13:13." Then I hung up.

Okay, it's beyond weird. Or even crazy, for that matter. Yes, it could even be considered downright creepy. But it must have worked — or Amy just felt so embarrassed for me that she agreed to go out.

Exactly thirteen months later we played the recording of that message as Amy walked down the aisle at our wedding. Our cake beautifully displayed our favorite Bible verse — the one born out of that very first call.

"I DO" ISN'T THE ANSWER

In our culture, most girls grow up fantasizing about the most special, life-changing day of their lives — their wedding day. The groom, of course, is Mr. Perfect — that ideal kind of guy combining the best qualities of Mr. Darcy, Mr. Big, and Mr. Brad Pitt. Following their dream wedding, only more perfection will follow. They'll purchase the cutest house, enjoy the most romantic life with Mr. Perfect, and have two beautiful kids, with wonderful names that she picked out back in first grade.

Most guys grow up and dream of marrying a gorgeous woman and having sex twice a day and three times on Sunday. They are all still dreaming.

When it comes to marriage and the kind of love required to forge such a bond, both women and men are very confused. Many believe that to really be fulfilled in life, you have to meet "the one" — your soul mate, your "eHarmony compatibility exact-match" partner, the only person who can complete you like no other, the one great love of a lifetime.

Sounds good … and it is true. Just not in the way most of us think. Such an ideal, and the many false expectations that come with it, is as timeless as love itself.

We can see the problem up close in a Bible story that rivals anything Jerry Springer could dream up. It's the twisted story of a guy named Jacob who becomes smitten by a beauty named Rachel. We're told, "Rachel was lovely in form, and beautiful" (Gen. 29:17) — the biblical way of saying she was smoking hot!

Maybe I'm reading into the story, but it's obvious that Jacob's life was empty. We know that he never enjoyed his father's approval, that he cheated his brother so outrageously that they became lifelong enemies, and that he "had issues with" his overprotective, manipulative mother. Seriously, *Days of Our Lives* has nothing on this story!

At this point in his life, like many of us, Jacob had no understanding of God's unconditional love. So when he saw this perfect ten of a woman alone at a well, it's easy to assume that his heart and mind raced in tandem: *If I can marry this breathtaking beauty, my life will be perfect and I'll be the guy all the other guys envy. If only I can have her, my life will matter! She will make me happy. I must have her at all costs!*

Sound familiar? Maybe you can relate. So many people don't feel valuable without a member of the opposite sex beside them. Girls and women are often encouraged and conditioned to think that they need a boyfriend or husband to feel attractive, complete, successful, worthy. *I need a man to feel special and loved.* They feel worthless unless there's a man — sometimes any man, including those who are unhealthy or abusive — at the center of their universe.

Similarly, many boys and men find their identity only by having a woman on their arm — and typically not just any woman but a knockout who will make everyone else notice when she walks into a room. One who will make people think, "He must be quite a man to be with her!" Middle-aged and older men seem especially vulnerable to their own fragile egos. Facing their own mortality and life's disappointments, they long to feel strong, handsome, virile, and successful again. They will often abandon their faithful wives for younger, more attractive women, with no more remorse than that of trading in last year's model for a new car. To these men, a beautiful woman is a necessary commodity to make them feel like a true man.

Like a lovesick teenager, Jacob believed that marrying Rachel would be the answer to all his problems. If he could only marry her, he wouldn't have to feel so empty, so lonely, so afraid, so uncertain, and so unsure of himself. Unfortunately, when you wrongly believe marriage is the answer — as Jacob did — you create a weak foundation upon which to build your relationship. Expecting that your spouse can meet all your needs and eliminate all struggles only sets you both up for three significant challenges: compromise, entitlement, and bitterness.

THREE STRIKES

When you view your spouse (or potential spouse) as your savior, you quickly become willing to compromise your standards. In Jacob's story, obsessed with his dream of marriage to lovely-in-form, smoking-hot Rachel, Jacob makes a bold and generous offer to her uncle: "I'll work for you seven years in return for your younger daughter Rachel" (Gen. 29:18). This seems like an odd proposal compared with our understanding of engagements and marriages today, but this wasn't unusual in Jacob's day. One thing does stand out, though. Jacob's bid for his bride was extravagant. He offered about four times more than the normal going price for a wife. He was so in love with the idea of love — at any cost — that he gave more than he should have.

Such blind devotion may strike us as immature, but self-compromise still happens all the time today. A young woman wants to wait until she's married to share the gift of lovemaking with her husband, but trying to maintain the attention of her boyfriend, she gives in and has sex. Or a guy adores his beloved so much that he dives deep into debt to prove his love: jewelry, clothes, fancy meals, maybe even a car. If and when they do get married, they're starting out with a huge financial burden and a precedent for buying affections. When you believe marriage is your answer, you'll often give something that eventually hurts you both.

Another problem with the obsession with relationships is that you'll become demanding. After working seven years, Jacob demanded his prize: "Give me my wife. My time is completed, and I want to lie with her" (Gen. 29:21). In the original language, this phrase "I want to lie with her" conveys a lustful, sexually charged demand — not a gentle invitation for the intimacy of marriage. Jacob's mindset was definitely focused on the marriage as a business transaction: "I did my part; now Laban had better do his, because I'm entitled to what's mine. I paid the price. Now I'd better get the goods."

Not a great way to start a marriage.

Yet we often see this mindset in many couples today, a transactional, "you owe me" attitude. It's totally normal for one spouse to feel like, "I did my part; now you do yours." "I bought you that new bracelet, so you'd better give me what I want, when I want it." "I made you dinner, so you'd better clean out the garage." "I work two jobs, so you should do all the housework."

We wrestle with this entitlement issue in our marriage. Amy home-schools our six kids and oversees our home — keeping it clean, organized, and well maintained. Since she works so hard, sometimes she feels like I owe her whatever she wants. Even when I'm exhausted, she still demands my body. Often I just want to cuddle and talk, but she has only one thing on her mind. I end up feeling cheap and used — like a piece of meat. (Okay, if you believe this, I have some beautiful swampland to sell you. Just making sure you are still paying attention.)

Finally, when marriage is your answer, you'll always end up disappointed and dissatisfied. It's normal today for people to enter marriage with so many expectations that no one on earth could possibly meet them all. So many couples are destined for a letdown before the marriage starts.

Our buddy Jacob discovers this firsthand. After receiving his nephew's seven-year payment, Laban starts thinking, "I have this young, beautiful daughter — Rachel — that any man on the planet would do anything to marry. But I also have an older Ugly Betty named Leah who may never even have a date, let alone a husband. Hmm, yes, I've got a plan."

So Laban pulls a switcheroo! After Jacob downs a little too much champagne at the reception, Laban enacts his plan and sends Leah, in wedding gown and heavy veil, into the honeymoon tent. Imagine the hangover Jacob has when he opens his eyes the next morning and finds out that his sister-in-law has become his wife! Enraged by Laban's cruel deception, Jacob nevertheless agrees to pay seven more years' labor to earn his beloved Rachel.

Again, not the best way to start a marriage. When you fall in love with an ideal, it becomes impossible not to be disappointed by the very human person beside you. Too often we set ourselves up to marry Rachel, our embodiment of perfection who can complete us and fulfill our every desire, and end up with the reality of Leah, a flesh-and-blood human being every bit as flawed as we are.

LOOKING FOR NUMBER TWO

Like Jacob, most normal people believe that to really be fulfilled in life, you have to find the one. This is true, but not as most people think. While it's normal to hear someone raving about their last date with "I think I've met the one!" it's much more unlikely to hear someone gush, "I think I just met the two of my life!"

Because it's true: to really be fulfilled in life, you have to meet the One. God is your one. And your spouse should be your two.

I'm not just trying to be corny or cute or clever — the Bible makes a clear case for this relational hierarchy. We're told to seek God *first* (Matt. 6:33). The *first* command of the Ten Commandments is to love God and not have idols. (When we seek marriage — and all it represents to us — more than God, marriage becomes an idol.) Jesus said the *first* and greatest command is to love God first, then love others next. God is our number one, and our spouse is our number two. If we focus on God first and view our spouse as his gift to us, we stop expecting another person to do what only God can do.

Putting God first does not guarantee that your marriage will be easy, only that it will be easier than struggling with compromise, entitlement, and bitterness. Just as the secret to dieting or debt-free living is amazingly simple yet overwhelmingly hard, so is the key to a healthy, wonderfully weird marriage. If you want your marriage to be better than normal, you must concentrate, communicate, and collaborate.

Years into marriage, most normal couples stop doing what made them close. Before long they coexist like roommates, sticking together for the sake of the kids. One woman told me that she thought being single was the loneliest phase of her life, until she was married to an unresponsive husband. Several men have told me that they slipped into emotional or physical affairs because they drifted away from emotional intimacy with their wives without even realizing it until they were lost at sea. Why do people who were once so much in love end up dividing possessions in divorce court? It's often because they stopped tending the garden together.

TEND THE GARDEN

Think about it: Is there any area of your life that you can stop working on and still see growth? Can you eat anything you want, avoid exercise, and expect to have a healthy body? Of course not. Can you let your front lawn go, never watering, fertilizing, or mowing, and expect to see a lush expanse of green beautiful enough to win the yard-of-the-month award? Again, forget it. Can you throw your money blindly into the stock market, never look at it again, and retire on your first investment? Not likely. And yet normal people neglect their marriage and expect it to thrive.

If the grass looks greener somewhere else, it's time to water your own lawn.

No wonder, then, that it can be so tempting to just cut your losses and repeat the cycle all over again. Statistically, the more times a person has been divorced, the higher the likelihood that his or her next marriage will end that way too. If the grass looks greener somewhere else, it's time to water your own lawn.

If you want to buck the norm and have what few have, do what few do — concentrate on your marriage as a living, growing garden that requires planting and tending, watering and weeding.

We see this from the beginning. In the garden of Eden, God created Adam and then Eve. God said that a man would leave his father and mother and be united to his wife and they would become one flesh (Gen. 2:24). The word translated as "united" is the Hebrew word *dabaq*. It means to cling or adhere, to catch by pursuit, to pursue hard with affection and devotion. Here's how this word is translated in other versions of the Bible. I'll highlight the words that come from *dabaq*.

> "I follow *close behind you*" (Ps. 63:8 TLB).
> "They are *joined fast* to one another; they cling together and
>   cannot be parted" (Job 41:17).
> "They … *pursued hard* after them" (Judg. 20:45 KJV).

We should continue to pursue our spouse with this same passion and fervor that we expressed when we were dating. Before marriage, couples will often pursue each other. Naturally, men generally will pursue their potential bride. Unfortunately, men are hunters. Once they make the kill (the marriage), some move on to hunt something else (typically a career or hobby). We can't let that happen to our relationships. It may seem weird to keep dating after you're married, but it will prevent you from settling for normal.

If you want to buck the norm and have what few have, do what few do.

It's not that most people want to have lame or painful marriages. In fact, I'm guessing that the majority of couples hope and plan for a rich and meaningful one. Each person probably has good intentions. But good intentions won't get you very far.

Have you noticed that we tend to judge others by their actions, but we judge ourselves by our intentions? This is especially true in marriage relationships.

If Amy forgot our anniversary (which would never happen — ever), I'd judge her actions and pronounce, "You don't care about me." But if I forgot, I'd try to defend myself: "Uh, I was going to do something special, but I just got busy — you remember that book I had to write? I really meant to take you away for a romantic weekend at the bed-and-breakfast you love, but I just forgot. You believe me, don't you?" To have a wonderfully different marriage, we've got to close the gap between intentions and actions.

Have you noticed that we tend to judge others by their actions, but we judge ourselves by our intentions?

JUST SAY THE WORD

Which brings us to communication. Again, a no-brainer essential ingredient to any healthy relationship. Yet in marriage, it takes effort to continue working on communication day after day, year after year. Ever notice those little mannerisms or gestures that only you and your spouse use to communicate? You know, when it's time to leave the party, the old tug on the left earlobe. These kinds of signals and shorthand come only with time and familiarity. But too often we allow these to replace specific, deliberate, meaningful communication.

If you are a man, it's especially helpful to pursue your wife with words of affection. Normal guys do this when they are dating but let it wane when married. Don't be normal. Woman especially need non-sexual affection. (Guys, you might wonder what that is, so I'll spell it out slowly: N-O-N-S-E-X-U-A-L A-F-F-E-C-T-I-O-N. This is affection without sexual strings attached. It does exist.) Many normal men often abandon verbal compliments after marriage. One of the most helpful things I've counseled men to do is to add one word to their expression of love: *because.*

The next time you say, "I love you," add this word: *because.* "I love you because ..." Then fill in the blank. Say something specific that is special to you. "I love you because you are so faithful." "I love you because you are my best friend." "I love you because you sacrificed your career to give us a family." "I love you because you have a great sense of humor."

Here's the key. Always add a *because* — but never repeat a reason. Be creative. And be sincere. Each time you say it, give her a different *because*.

Ladies, just as you need to be affirmed with words of affection, your man needs to be affirmed with words of affirmation. He may seem confident to many, but most men (including me) are pathetically insecure. We live in a world that drills into us, "You are only as good as your last accomplishment." If you were the top sales guy last month, what are you going to do this month? If you made a good presentation at the last board meeting, can you top it at the next one? If you made 20 percent on your last project, can you make 25 percent on the next one? For men, our self-worth often evaporates with our last accomplishment.

In so many ways, a husband is in the process of becoming what his wife sees in him. Since she knows him better than anyone else, if she says he's no good, he's tempted to believe it. If she thinks he's amazing, he'll start to believe he can accomplish a lot. (You might not believe in him as much as you used to. If he is less than you want, your lack of faith — though merited — is not going to help. Whatever you can affirm — do!)

In my line of work, there are a lot of critics. It's pretty easy to take shots at a pastor for any number of different reasons. Without an encouraging wife, I could easily become discouraged and doubt myself. But because the woman who knows me most intimately believes in me (and tells me often), I can shake off the negative voices and continue to do great things.

For men, our self-worth often evaporates with our last accomplishment.

Ladies, you'll probably want to know, "Does he love me today?" (Men, tell her and tell her why.) At the same time, men want to know, "Do you believe in me today?" (Ladies, tell him.)

Finally, if you want to improve the quality of your marriage in a weird way, surprise your spouse by helping without being asked, nagged, or told. I've discovered through trial and many errors that one of the most romantic things to do for a woman is to help her. That's right! I didn't say bring flowers or chocolate (although that's good too). I'm talking about good old-fashioned get in there and do something useful. Vacuum the carpet. Wipe the table. Fold the clothes. Bathe the kids. Unload the dishwasher.

One of the most loving things that Amy does for me is to totally take care of the kids on the weekends so I can focus on preaching. She literally does everything so I can prayerfully prepare. With the hectic pace of our lives, it can be easy to feel sorry for ourselves and think, "If she only knew what kind of day I had at work today" or "If he only knew what a circus it was today trying to clean the carpets, keep the kids outside, and pay the bills." So we normally end up feeling justified when we ignore, postpone, or refuse to help out. Marriage requires serving the one you love with the selfless love of Christ. This includes acts of service, working together, even when it's not easy or convenient.

> **A husband is in the process of becoming what his wife sees in him.**

Remember, to get what you've never had, you must do what you've never done. But to get what you once had, you must do what you once did. Jesus said to the church in Ephesus in Revelation 2:5, "Remember the height from which you have fallen! Repent and do the things you did at first." In marriage, I know there are some who need to repent — to apologize — and to do the things they did at first.

If you're married today, chances are that at some point back in the past you had something pretty special. What happened? Chances are pretty good that you slipped into a normal trap, and life squeezed out all the things that made your relationship work.

Think for a moment about what you used to do and start doing it again. Maybe you need to watch *Top Gun* together and memorize cheesy lines. Maybe you need to just have fun and laugh together. Maybe you need to talk about what you've been afraid to say.

It might feel weird at first, but stick with it. Weird is good. Normal isn't working. I pray that God blesses you with a wonderfully weird marriage.

Chapter 8

AIMING AT THE WRONG TARGET

Don't worry that children never listen to you; worry that they are always watching you.

— ROBERT FULGHUM

One evening my daughter Catie came bursting into our bedroom to tattle on her little sister. "Mommy and Daddy!" She rushed to get the words out. "Mandy said a really *really* bad word!" Accustomed to drama, Amy and I calmly asked her to tell us the really *really* bad word. Mandy's older sister stalled. "It's so bad, I can't say it," she explained soberly. Leaning in some, Amy asked, "Catie, can you tell me what letter the word started with?" The distressed tattler leaned in and whispered, "Mommy, Mandy said B.S."

Since Mandy was only six at the time, this got our attention. Trying not to show panic, we wondered where she heard that expression. Amy calmly said to Catie, "I promise you that you won't get in trouble, but can you please tell me what B.S. stands for?" At first Catie resisted. After continuous prodding, she whispered ever so softly, "Everyone knows that B.S. stands for Britney Spears."

To this day, we can't decide if we should be proud of that story or incredibly embarrassed. Either way, we laugh every time we tell it.

MIDDLE GROUND

As a pastor for more than twenty years, I've encountered a variety of families and parenting styles. From very traditional families with Dad as the sole breadwinner, Mom as the stay-at-homemaker, and two kids (often a girl and a boy — who look like Mini-Me's of their parents) to single-parent families where the mom or the dad has to shoulder all the responsibility of raising their children. I've met families that combined races, either through adoption or the parents' ethnicity, and blended families that could give the Brady Bunch a run for their money. No matter how diverse the family appears from the outside, though, I've discovered that almost every parent struggles with the same core issues about how to raise their children.

Someone might argue, "Craig, don't you think you might have sheltered your kids too much if one of them thinks B.S. stands for Britney Spears?" You might have a point. Because let's face it, when it comes to parenting, most people don't want to raise odd or socially awkward kids. And we certainly don't want rebellious heathens who do jail time for selling drugs before they're old enough to vote. Rather than being overly permissive or legalistically strict, we typically find comfort blending in, parenting like most of those around us.

Sure, a few families drift to the edges, the extremes. (You often see the extreme oddballs on *Wife Swap*.) One family homeschools their kids and doesn't let them watch any television, eat junk food, play with friends, or know what is going on in the real world.

We want to protect our kids, but we don't want to be weird like that.

At the same time, we're not on the other edge either. Some lenient parents allow their thirteen-year-old daughters to car date and their fifteen-year-old sons to surf porn on the internet. (Their dad does too, and he's not a rapist or anything.) These families have no rules and no boundaries. Some might argue that they don't even have parents, because the parents are more friends or buddies than authority figures.

We love our kids and want to give them freedom, but not so much that it harms them.

Some parents are old-fashioned and make their kids work — almost like slaves. Their kids rise early, fall in line, say "yes sir" and "yes ma'am," and work for everything they have.

While we might believe in hard work, we don't want to torture our kids. After all, we want them to have a childhood.

Then there's the other extreme. Rather than working their kids, some parents spoil them rotten. Their princes and princesses never lift a finger. If they want Rock and Republic jeans, their parents get them two pairs. If they want a phone, they don't get the free one; they get the latest iPhone with the unlimited data plan. On their sixteenth birthday, they get a car nicer than their teachers at school can afford.

Of course we love our kids and want to provide for them, but we don't want to spoil them like some parents spoil their kids.

Most people, even Christians, tend to avoid these extremes and instead drift toward the center. Comparisons help us feel more comfortable. Since we're good parents, we stay away from those bad edges. We don't shelter our kids too much. We don't give them too much freedom. We strive not to be too demanding. And we never want to make them into entitled, no-good, lazy brats. So we stay away from the edges and we shoot for the middle of the road.

The problem is, we're aiming for the middle of the wrong target.

WHAT IN THE WORLD?

If you asked most parents what they want for their kids, you'd get some variation of the following statements: "I just want my Brandon and Kendra to enjoy their lives." "Since Johnny's on the traveling soccer team, we're hoping he plays college soccer one day." "We're just trying to give Ginger and Gabe more opportunities than we had." "I hope Bethany gets a good education and then a high-paying job." "We're praying that Ketric stays away from the wrong crowd so he doesn't get sucked into bad things." "If Shannon studies hard, I think she can get into medical school. That would be a dream come true." "Keisha keeps bringing home bad boys. We just hope she marries a good man."

None of these are bad wishes for our children. In fact, they are all pretty good. If that's the bull's-eye and your kids hit it, you might be pretty happy. Most normal people would be.

But God didn't call us to be dead in the center of what the world calls success. In fact, if our kids are successful in every normal way, they can still miss God's main mark. Jesus said, "What good is it for a man to gain the whole world, and yet lose or forfeit his very self?" (Luke 9:25). If we raise our children to become well-adjusted, materially comfortable, professionally successful adults, but they don't know the One who created them or live for him, then all the success in the world is for nothing. Psalm 127 tells us that sons are like arrows in the hands of a warrior. What if we're pointing our arrows in the wrong direction?

Normal is to strive for the center of what the world lives like.

Weird is to live to be in the center of God's will.

THE CENTER OF GOD'S WILL

We have to understand that when it comes to parenting, there are no guarantees. Sometimes great Christian parents raise strong Christian kids. On the other hand, I've watched very strong and committed Christian parents raise kids who eventually became complete hellions. (Growing up, I always heard that preachers' kids were the wildest.) At the same time, I've seen tremendous Christians emerge from families that didn't resemble anything godly. Surefire parenting formulas don't exist. But even though there are no guarantees, there are certain biblical principles that we aim at.

Instead of trying to lead our children to be like those around them, we should lead them to be like Christ. Romans 12:2 in the Message version says, "Don't become so well-adjusted to your culture that you fit into it without even thinking. Instead, fix your attention on God. You'll be changed from the inside out. Readily recognize what he wants from you, and quickly respond to it. Unlike the culture around you, always dragging you down to its level of immaturity, God brings the best out of you, develops well-formed maturity in you."

When Jesus invested in his disciples (or we could say raised God's children), he certainly challenged them to be different and set apart, but he never told them to hide in a cave to stay safe. In fact, when Jesus came, he came full of grace and truth (John 1:14). As parents, when we lead with all grace, our permissiveness could allow our children to wander into dangerous places and take in harmful influences. On the other hand, when we constantly deliver heavy-handed truth, our dogmatic parenting can produce legalistic kids who are later prone to rebel. Like Jesus, we must parent with grace and truth.

What the neighbor kids do isn't our standard of right and wrong. What the kids on the volleyball team do doesn't define our standard of truth. The morals of the kids on *The Real World* don't drive us. Though it is unquestionably weird, God's Word should be one guardrail in life. It protects us from running off the road into dangerous temptation. While some consider God's standards as too confining, a true believer sees them as loving and freeing.

Yet parenting and communicating truth are only half the equation. The other guardrail is grace. Since our kids are human, they will mess up. And when they do, they need the same love and grace that God shows us.

Many studies and surveys have documented the way so many kids graduate from high school and then let their faith slide or dissolve altogether in college. A recent survey by America's Research Group revealed that 95 percent of evangelical Christians aged twenty to twenty-nine attended church regularly during their elementary and middle school years. However, 55 percent attended church in high school and only 11 percent were still attending in college.[5]

So the problem is not just leaving home and having the freedom to sleep in and skip church. It seems more likely that kids may not be experiencing the relevancy of church or seeing the significance of their faith in light of what they experience at school and at home. And these are Christian kids. Which tells us that even when we homeschool and do everything in our power to build them into strong believers, somehow we don't seem to be equipping them very well.

So how do we become weird (or weirder) parents? Not by pretending to be perfect and have all the answers. Instead, we must let them see our struggles as well as our strengths. Weird parents not only try to mirror God's character on a daily basis but also show their humanity — their own questions, doubts, weaknesses — in the mix. They share answered prayers as well as the unanswered ones. They lose their tempers — and then are humble enough to ask for forgiveness. Being a good parent is impossible unless we rely on God for strength, patience, guidance, wisdom, and discernment — and teach our kids how to do the same.

One time when Amy was running late, our whole family loaded into our Suburban a full twenty-three minutes behind schedule. (When you're mad, you quote exact minutes. It's not twenty or twenty-five minutes; it's twenty-three!) Extremely frustrated that we'd be tardy for an important meeting, I punched the gas pedal and raced the Suburban like it was a Mustang GT. When Amy told me to slow down, rebelliously I sped up. After missing a turn, I wheeled the car around (like something from *The Dukes of Hazzard*) and did a 180 in the middle of a four-lane street. The kids all flew toward the side window and screamed in fear. When I straightened our vehicle, the whole car was silent. No one spoke. No one moved. No one breathed.

Finally my oldest daughter, who was twelve at the time, said, "Daddy, you need to pull this car over, and Mom needs to give you a hard spanking."

She was right. Pastor/Daddy/Spiritual-Man-of-God had just acted like a total you-know-what. The only thing I could do was fall on my sword and ask for forgiveness. "Daddy messed up really bad. I'm so sorry. What I did was wrong. Will you please forgive me?" I said with my tail between my legs.

Of course they all forgave me, and they retell the "Dad needs a spanking" story to all their friends. But more important, they extended the same grace to me that I've extended to them. They know I'm not perfect, nor do I pretend to be. But they do know that I love God and want to please him. When I don't, I do what we all should do and ask for his help and forgiveness.

We become weirder parents when we fall more and more in love with Christ. When we become like him, we'll exhibit his nature. Rather than imposing our standards (or lack of standards) on our children, we'll model a growing-Christlike life.

When I asked my oldest son what he wanted to do when he grew up, I beamed with pride when he said, "Dad, I want to do what you do." "You want to be a preacher," I said enthusiastically, imagining him as a chip off the old block. "No, Daddy," Sam said. "When I grow up, I want to be like you — the best dad in the world."

I want to be like my heavenly Father, because my son wants to be like me.

DECLARATION OF INDEPENDENCE

Just recently our youngest daughter, Jojo, told me she was ready to throw away her "little-girl training wheels." After teaching five other kids to ride their bikes, I felt a mixture of joy and sadness, knowing this would be my last round of running alongside a scared but trusting child, cheering her into her first solo ride, soon followed by her first and inevitable fall.

"Don't drop me, Daddy!" Jojo squealed with excitement as she pedaled down our driveway. "Daddy's got you," I assured her. "Daddy's got you."

Within a few minutes she weaved and wobbled, beginning to get the hang of it. Loosening my grip, I stayed close, running step-by-step alongside my baby rider.

It seems like yesterday that I held her in my arms in the hospital. I blinked. When I opened my eyes, she was five years old and riding her pink Barbie bicycle down the driveway — all by herself — shouting, "I can do it by myself! I don't need you, Daddy. I don't need you!"

I loved hearing those words and I despised them — all at the same time.

As parents, we sometimes find ourselves stumbling through life on autopilot — simply trying to make it through one day at a time. So maybe we should back up a moment and start with clarifying our role as parents.

Our greatest priority as Christian parents is to gradually transfer our children's dependence away from us until it rests solely on God.

Obviously, we have high hopes for our children, but we're not sure how to help them achieve godly dreams. To have your kids end up somewhere on purpose, start with the destination in mind. To do so, you'll need to be able to clearly articulate your number one priority as a parent — and consistently reinforce it by what you do.

What is priority one? I believe our greatest priority as Christian parents is to gradually transfer our children's dependence away from us until it rests solely on God. Simple though it sounds, helping your kids move gracefully (with grace — fully) from childhood into adulthood is a profoundly challenging lifetime calling.

Early in life, our children depend on us, as parents, for everything. They can't eat without us, find their crib without us, get dressed without us, or change their diapers without us. Before long, if we do our jobs, they can feed themselves, dress themselves, go to the bathroom by themselves, and get ready for bed by themselves. (If you have toddlers, be encouraged! There is hope!)

If we are faithful parents, we gradually teach our children to do things without us. But our goal should not be to raise totally independent kids. Our goal is to raise them to be dependent — not on us or anyone else but on the true Lord God. He is the only one who knows what's best for them and can lead them to his perfect will. Above all else, we should — over time — teach our children what it means and what it looks like to depend on God.

Deuteronomy 6 highlights this truth: "These are the commands, decrees and laws the LORD your God directed me to teach you to observe in the land that you are crossing the Jordan to possess, so that you, your children and their children after them may fear the LORD your God as long as you live" (vv. 1 – 2). This is not a quick homework review for Tuesday's geography quiz. This is a PhD in lifelong learning about how to impart God's truth and commands to our children. This kind of education should rank infinitely higher than a perfect score on the spelling test, scoring two goals in a hockey game, or playing first chair flute.

No matter how often we acknowledge this as our top priority, it is really hard to live out. And if we are not intentional about imparting a spiritual legacy to our children, I can promise you that our spiritual enemy is plotting full-time how he can divert our kids from God's best to anything destructive. Unfortunately, his method often involves diverting us from our heart's desire by getting us to settle for what's normal instead of pursuing God's best.

Our goal is not to raise kids who can endure R-rated movies and still be productive teenagers, or sheltered children who think Britney Spears is a cuss word. Instead, we pray that our children will grow to not need us but instead need and intimately know God, then on their own — in his grace and truth — have the strength to say no to dangerous influences and temptation and live with the grace to love those who don't live the truth they embrace.

ORGANIC PARENTING

The best thing you can do for your kids is to show them God working in you on a daily basis. I love the practical teaching of Deuteronomy 6:6 – 9: "These commandments that I give you today are to be upon your hearts. Impress them on your children. Talk about them when you sit at home and when you walk along the road, when you lie down and when you get up. Tie them as symbols on your hands and bind them on your foreheads. Write them on the doorframes of your houses and on your gates."

You can do all these things God's Word encourages us to do. They can become a part of how you do life — in fact, they are only really effective if they're a consistent part of everyday life. Kids are quick to pick up on our real feelings and motives, so the only way to be a truly weird, life-changing parent is to express your faith organically.

Talk about God with your kids in the morning on the way to school, let them know when you pray for them during their day, and share a meaningful truth from Scripture on the way home from dance. Put a favorite Bible verse on the wall alongside Miley Cyrus and Justin Bieber. Let them know the hardest part of your day, as appropriate for their age, and how you connect it back to your trust in God. Make spiritual conversations a part of how you do life.

You could do this in any number of ways. For our family, we make the evening dinner a daily party. (With eight people, every meal is a party.) On good days, everyone is involved in preparing the meal. (And no one leaves until the kitchen is clean.) At the table, we start with prayer. And every evening, each family member shares a high point of the day. And in all high points, we celebrate God's goodness. From there our conversations naturally flow into sharing Bible verses and spiritual discussions.

Unfortunately, it's all too normal to separate spiritual life from regular life. In reality, there is no distinction. Everything we do is spiritual. Studying for a test, playing T-ball, going to Grandma and Grandpa's house — we need God in all those moments and places, that last one especially if you have six kids and a dog in a Suburban. While normal people separate life into compartments (school, home, sports, work, friends — and oh yeah, church and the spiritual stuff), weird people know that everything is spiritual. We don't remember God in prayer at the end of the day. We live aware of God moment by moment. He is not a part of our lives; God is our life.

CRAIG'S LIST

If we're not to be too permissive with our kids nor too restrictive, how do we find the wonderfully weird sweet spot? Proverbs 22:6 says, "Train a child in the way he should go, and when he is old he will not turn from it." The Hebrew word translated here as "train" is *chanak*, which means to initiate, dedicate, or teach. We should not scold, manipulate, or try to control our kids. Instead, we're striving to train them according to God's Word. Training is an active, dynamic process lived out daily in all areas of life — not a rote exercise in memorizing verses and going to church every week.

Proverbs contains so much wisdom for parents. From this book, Amy and I have gleaned seven key areas that form much of our focus for training our kids to learn God's ways in today's world. Since many of them are explored in greater detail, or even have their own chapters, elsewhere in this book, I'll just give you a quick Craig's list:

1. *Train them to manage God's money (Prov. 3:9 – 10).* I've mentioned this before but cannot overstate how important it is to train the next generation in financial responsibility. They are the most "entitled" generation in our country's history — probably because they've seen our generation borrow to buy whatever we want *now*! Delayed gratification and wise stewardship will benefit them for a lifetime.

2. *Train them to carefully select friends (Prov. 13:20).* The Bible is clear: bad company corrupts good morals (1 Cor. 15:33). The right friends can make or break a child. We may not always be able to control the kind of peer pressure exerted on our kids in various situations, but we can influence how they choose and interact with their friends into adulthood.

3. *Train them to watch their words (Prov. 4:24).* Out of the overflow of our hearts our mouths speak (Luke 6:45). If our words are not

honoring to God or to people, we have a heart issue that will ripple throughout so many other areas and relationships. Words have enormous power — particularly the ones we as parents use with our kids. Teach them to speak words of life and not destruction.

4. *Train them to be responsible (Prov. 6:6 – 8).* We've chosen not to give our kids an allowance for doing nothing. They have chores they are expected to do. Outside of their chores, they can earn money for doing various other jobs. You might feel like you're doing them a favor by giving them an allowance simply for showing up, or buying them whatever they ask for, but ultimately you could be handicapping them for the rest of their lives.

5. *Train them to guard their minds (Prov. 23:7).* Our thoughts shape our emotions, our decisions, and our actions. How we think, and what we think about, directs our lives. While it is normal to be plagued with negative self-talk, we're trying to help our children learn the skill of capturing wrong thoughts and making them obedient to Christ (2 Cor. 10:5).

6. *Train them to be generous (Prov. 11:25).* By nature, we are selfish. (Have you spent time with a two-year-old lately? Can you say, "Mine!") Yet we are never more like God than when we give. Generosity is a gift that can be nurtured. A generous person will always be blessed.

7. *Train them to fear God (Prov. 1:7).* It's normal today for people to live without respecting and revering God. But we know that the fear of God is the beginning of wisdom (Ps. 111:10). If we don't fear God, it's because we don't know God.

Parenting is one of the hardest, grittiest, richest, most glorious gifts that God entrusts to us. To love our children well, which virtually every parent innately longs to do, requires us to choose the narrow path that lies between the easier, broader gates of all or nothing. God created us as his unique, individual children and loves us accordingly, in ways we can't even imagine. He loves us enough to give us the free will to choose how we respond to him and his love. We're not robots, droids, clones, or accidents.

We must love our children with the same combination of devotion and autonomy, balancing grace and truth. It's normal to neglect our kids by default by working sixty-hour to seventy-hour weeks. It's normal to indulge them with everything the world can offer — or to withhold it all. It's normal to be so terrified of messing up their lives and our own that we fail sometimes.

But we're called to be wonderfully weird parents: moms and dads who engage with their kids, fully in the present moments of each day. Parents who navigate with their kids through the currents of culture, using the compass of God's Word. Parents who overcome their fear with love, which is my definition of courage. And also my definition of weird.

Chapter 9

IF YOU
PLEASE

The art of pleasing is the art of deceiving.

— OLD FRENCH PROVERB

When I was growing up, the labels on your clothes determined your destiny. They indicated who sat at the cool table in the cafeteria and who didn't. They revealed who had enough money to afford designer clothes from the mall stores instead of clothes off the clearance rack at Walmart. The right labels revealed who was hip enough to know the latest trends and styles, what was in and what (and who) was out.

When I was in middle school, those who were in wore Izod, the brand more widely known today as Lacoste. You can instantly recognize this classic brand by the unmistakable alligator symbol always positioned perfectly on each shirt or garment. Every cool kid in my school sported the expensive gators — except me.

It wasn't that my parents didn't appreciate my fashion dilemma. They always wanted to give me the best. However, we simply couldn't afford those high-priced reptiles. Hoping to solve the problem and provide my ticket for lunch at the cool table, Mom devised an ingenious plan.

She searched and searched until she finally found the prize: a pair of Izod socks at a garage sale. For a mere quarter, she purchased not one but two matching alligators (that just happened to be attached to the socks), each one precisely the same size as their more expensive siblings on the coveted Izod shirts. From a nearby discount store, she picked up a cheap polo shirt, and then she surgically removed one prized gator from a sock and transplanted it to the label-less polo.

The next day, I strutted into class wearing my wannabe Izod shirt, doubly proud since it had cost about one-tenth the price of a real one. By second hour, however, my friend Travis noticed that my reptile was tilted just a bit off-kilter and immediately shouted, "Hey, look at this — Groeschel's wearing a *fake* Izod!" Despite my mom's best efforts, my crooked crocodile gave me away. Needless to say, the Milli Vanilli lip-sync scandal was nothing compared to the infamous Groeschel Izod incident.

THE DISEASE TO PLEASE

During adolescence, the relentless need to belong and fit in with our peers can drive us to extreme measures — often more harmful than my fake gator humiliation. Many people first experiment with alcohol, drugs, and premarital sex in their teens just to feel

When we place the approval of other people ahead of doing what we know will please our Father, we're creating a false idol.

normal, to feel that they belong. Research shows that teens without a strong family identity or a role in a positively focused group — such as a sports team or choir — are more susceptible to doing whatever it takes to fit in with any group that will have them.

Unfortunately, wanting to please our peers and doing whatever it takes to fit in don't end in our teens. We all want to feel like we're part of the right group — whoever we identify with or, more likely, want to be identified with. It's human nature to want to find our tribe and be recognized by them. The problem arises, however, when we're willing to compromise in two vital areas: (1) our relationship with God and (2) our relationship with ourselves.

As we've seen in a variety of contexts, God wants to be first in our lives — before money, our spouse, anyone, or anything. When we place the approval of other people ahead of doing what we know will please our Father, we're creating a false idol. Not only does it impair our ability to know God, but also it sends us on a wild-goose chase for a golden egg that doesn't exist. If the approval of others is all we live for, it will never be enough.

We also lose something else in pursuit of this illusion: respect for ourselves and consistency of character. If we repeatedly choose to act in ways that contradict our beliefs and values, we undermine our own authenticity and integrity. Or as Paul expresses it in his letter to the Romans, "What I don't understand about myself is that I decide one way, but then I act another, doing things I absolutely despise" (7:15 MSG). We end up compartmentalizing fragments of our lives and then wondering why we don't feel whole.

Once again I speak from experience. When I was in my early twenties, my senior pastor got sick and asked me to preach that week. It happened to be the first Sunday of the month, when we regularly celebrated the Lord's Supper together as a church community. I immediately experienced the familiar feeling of fear mingled with excitement, since I'd never done a Communion service before.

Before the service started, I positioned myself by the front door of the church to greet people as they entered. While I nodded and smiled in welcome, my thoughts blossomed with the fruit of insecurity: *How will it go today? Do these people even like me? Will I be able to win them over if they don't? Will I do a good job? Will I be funny in the right places and spiritual enough in all the others? Will my pastor approve and be proud?*

I greeted an elderly lady coming up the stairs into the sanctuary, and noticing her arduous climb, I darted down to assist her. As I helped her ascend the stairs, she commented on how much she loved our senior pastor's preaching. I agreed and then informed her that he wasn't feeling well and wouldn't be preaching that day. Mrs. Williams then stopped abruptly and turned to ask, "Then who is preaching?"

"I am!" I said enthusiastically, knowing she'd be impressed that I had helped her up the steps.

"Would you help me down the stairs and back to my car, then? I think I'm going to skip church today."

Double ouch. If this sweet little old lady doesn't want to hear my preaching, then no one will. My mind flooded with twice as many doubts as before. It was time for the service to begin, though, so there was no backing out.

On top of Mrs. Williams's vote of confidence, I had to conduct Communion for the first time. Nervous over who was going to dash out the door next, I was grateful that the long robe I was wearing (our church's traditional pastoral garb) covered my shaky legs. I told myself to just keep going and get it over with.

In my best pastoral manner, I dramatically lifted the Communion bread above my head toward heaven. Lowering my spiritually authoritative voice, I proclaimed, "This is Christ's body, which was broken for you." As the words flowed, my confidence grew and I thought, *This is going well — I can do this.*

Grasping the large cracker of matza bread carefully with both hands, I broke off a piece, held it in the air, and said, "Take, eat, the body of Christ." After serving myself Communion, I would then begin offering it to the congregation. The only problem was that what should have been a small corner of the cracker was more like half a box of saltines.

I panicked. Instead of a small, bite-size portion, I held a cracker big enough to feed a kindergarten class. Not wanting to break again the bread that symbolized Christ's body (and make it clear that I didn't know what I was doing), I quickly shoved it in my mouth. *Feels like sand in my throat,* I thought, wondering what to do next.

I'd obviously bitten off more than I could chew. (Extra points if you saw that coming.) My eyes started to water as the Sunday crowd stared silently at the spectacle before them. Fear gripped me. *How will I ever get this cracker down? What if I can't? Everyone is going to make fun of me! Man, how do I get into these situations? What a loser! My pastor will hear about this, and I'll never get to serve Communion again.*

Unable to get a full breath, I was aware that my red face was starting to turn purple. I had no choice but to try to gulp down the driest cracker known to man as quickly as possible. *Chew and swallow, just chew and swallow,* I told myself while the congregation couldn't decide whether to snicker or perform the Heimlich.

It was about to go from bad to worse.

Suddenly the body of Christ couldn't decide if it was going to go down or come back up. Certain that in two thousand years of Christian history, no one had ever vomited up the body of our Lord and Savior, I reached for the only drink available to keep him down — which turned out to be, you guessed it, his blood. Or at least the grape juice representing his blood. *Gulp.* I quickly washed down my mouthful of cracker, took a deep breath, and said, "Once again I've been saved by the blood!"

The congregation erupted in laughter and applause.

THE NEXT AMERICAN IDOL

Thankful that I'd avoided the first Communion death in history, I was proud of my clever spontaneity that had saved the day and won the crowd. It didn't take long, however, to realize that I was far more concerned with what the people thought than with what God thought.

I was far more concerned with what the people thought than with what God thought.

I'd known for some time that I was prone to pleasing people, but feeling the rush of adrenaline and hearing the explosion of applause that Sunday made me realize that I could easily become addicted to it, if I wasn't already.

Author Harriet Braiker, in her book *The Disease to Please*, reaches my same conclusion that people pleasing is actually a form of addiction. Just as a drug addict seeks drugs, people pleasers seek approval. She identifies four characteristic symptoms of Pleasers, and I identified with them all: (1) a tendency to take criticism personally, (2) a constant fear of rejection from those around them, (3) difficulty in expressing their true feelings, and (4) reluctance to say no even when it's clear they should. Any of these sound familiar to you?

Most of us wrestle with an occasional bout of the disease to please. Ironically, we often fail to see that whenever we compromise ourselves to please others, we tend to lose their respect. If people know you will do whatever it takes to placate them, make them happy, or avoid conflict, many if not most will exploit this as a weakness. When it's clear that we have a commitment to God that comes before anything else in our lives, most people will respect us even if they don't share our faith.

People pleasing is more of a spiritual problem than a relational problem.

To grow out of this dangerous disease, we've got to understand that people pleasing is more of a spiritual problem than a relational problem. Though most people would try to accept the need to please others as a normal part of life, we have to embrace that people pleasing is a form of idolatry. We have to be weird enough not to care what people think of who we are and how we live. Living for others' opinions is putting people ahead of God.

I remember clearly doing this a year or so after becoming a Christian. Before my transformation, partying was as normal as a mosquito hovering over a pond in Louisiana. After meeting Christ, though, I became convinced that for me, drinking's tagalong sins had to go. After some initial false starts, I finally eliminated alcohol from my life permanently — or so I thought.

While I was visiting California with some buddies, we stopped by a friend's home. That evening, my buddy (who didn't share my newfound passion for sobriety) invited some young ladies to join us for a few drinks. A few became more like the open bar at Larry King's last wedding. In no time everyone was drunk — except for the goody-two-shoes party pooper from Oklahoma.

The cutest girl from the bunch kept staring at me awkwardly, giving me that don't-I-know-you look. The beer must have really blurred her vision, because suddenly she shouted, "Tom Cruise! That's it — you look like Tom Cruise!" All the other girls laughed and hooted and soon started singing, "You've Lost That Lovin' Feeling." The pretty one handed me a beer, smiled, and said, "Have a drink with me, Tom."

Yes, it *is* amazing the impact that *Top Gun* has had on my life. Suddenly I was Tom Cruise and the cute drunk girl was Kelly McGillis. I drank one beer. One turned to two. Two turned to too many. I had compromised my values — all to please a drunk stranger I never saw again.

This people pleasing problem has haunted people throughout history. In John's gospel, the most religious people of the day — the Pharisees — regularly lived for public opinion rather than to please God. Whether it was praying long and showy prayers or bragging about a fast to look superspiritual, these posers were obsessed with public opinion. And some of the followers of Jesus were sucked into their people pleasing ploys. John 12:42 – 43 says, "Because of the Pharisees they would not confess their faith for fear they would be put out of the synagogue; for *they loved praise from men more than praise from God*" (emphasis mine).

KNOW FEAR

The fear of God is the only cure for the fear of people.

Like the Pharisees, are you afraid of what people will think if you don't go with the flow? Do you find yourself doing things you know you shouldn't because you want to be popular, liked, or approved? Do you feel the pressure to conform to a certain lifestyle, image, or role when you're around certain people you admire? There's only one solution to this problem, one antidote to the poison of pleasing.

The fear of God is the only cure for the fear of people.

If you've surrendered to normal living rather than the wonderful weirdness of being set apart by God, chances are that people are too big in your life and God is too small. Psalm 34:9 says, "Let the LORD's people show him reverence, for those who honor him will have all they need" (NLT). Reverence means a fear or awe. Those who know God will fear him — in the best sort of way, not like an escaped convict on the run from the law.

Maybe you already think of God as some kind of a cosmic cop, lurking to catch you breaking some commandment so he can arrest you and throw you in a cell in hell. If this is your concept of God, fearing him makes all the sense in the world. However, this image does not accurately reflect God's character, and fearing him is not about cowering like a dog from the pound. If you study the phrase "fear of God" in its original language, you'll discover that it actually means a reverent awe. It's this holy sense of "divine wow." Sometimes I experience such a moment of overwhelming respect, appreciation, and gratitude when I stand before a beautiful scene in the natural world. The grandeur and majesty of the Grand Canyon. The breathtaking vista of thousands of white diamonds glistening in the Colorado night sky, far away from the dull glow of urban lights. The brilliant gold-red-orange sunset kissing the ocean's horizon.

Take a moment to meditate on your own moments like this. God is the artist who created such scenes, not some angry cop out to slap you with a speeding ticket. Our heavenly Father is creator and sustainer of the universe. He is all knowing, all powerful, and ever present. He is so holy that mortals cannot look upon him in his purest essence and live. The same God who spoke everything into existence knew you before you were formed in your mother's womb. He is simultaneously the Alpha and the Omega, the beginning and the end, and the intimate lover of your soul.

He knows every hair on your head, and he sees every tear you shed. He is the great "I Am." He is called a consuming fire, the rock, the shelter, the hiding place, the healer, the provider. He is the God who loved you so much that his Son stripped himself of all heavenly glory to live as an impoverished Jewish carpenter so he could shed his blood, suffer, and die for the forgiveness of our sins. He is a God beyond description — and he loves us.

Pure, unadulterated *awe*.

Think of it this way. If you ride the biggest roller coaster in the world, the kids' ride at the county fair won't scare you. If you live through a hurricane and a tornado, a spring rain won't intimidate you. And when you truly know the God of the universe, people's opinions will no longer hold you hostage. Everything that once controlled you quickly loses all its power. Even winning the coveted title of All Greek Man of the Year.

GREEK TO ME

Even when I was still an undergraduate, I could have earned an honorary doctorate in people pleasing. As I shared earlier, between my sophomore year and junior year, although I'd been wholly consumed with being popular and accepted, suddenly I was drawn toward God. When I finally surrendered to God through Christ, everything changed. Instead of being normal, to my friends I instantly became weird. But since I was no longer a friend to the world, for the first time in my life, I could be a friend of God's.

Right before graduation, I had been nominated for All Greek Man of the Year. As meaningless as that award seems now, at the time it was a big deal to me. One of the many requirements to win was completing a detailed questionnaire that would be assessed by seven professors and college administrators before they made the final selection.

When I saw the last question on the form, I instantly froze: "What is the most important thing you've learned in your time at this university?" Without a doubt, the most important thing I learned involved knowing who Jesus really is and what he wanted for

I can't please everyone. But I can please God. Why work so hard to be normal, when God created you to stand out?

my life. But to answer it so honestly was clearly award-winning suicide. None of the decision makers were Christians. Most were probably even biased against Christians.

I agonized over my response. Should I craft a politically correct answer and cling to my chance to win? Or should I boldly tell the truth and forfeit any hope of the coveted award?

So I did what I knew I had to do, savoring a kind of divine satisfaction as I slowly penned the words, "The ... most ... important ... thing ... I ... learned ... is ... that ... Jesus ... Christ ... is ... the ... Lord ... of ... Lords. My ... life ... belongs ... to ... him."

It was so clear and simple after I recalled Paul's words to the Galatian believers: "Obviously, I'm not trying to be a people pleaser! No, I am trying to please God. If I were still trying to please people, I would not be Christ's servant" (Gal. 1:10 NLT).

On that day in college, I decided not to be a people pleaser. If I was still consumed with pleasing people, I could not be a fully devoted servant of Christ, which is what my heart desired most. Even more than being All Greek Man of the Year.

You might wonder, "Craig, did you win the award or not?" Sorry, but I'm not going to tell you. It truly doesn't matter.

Winning any award isn't nearly as important as living with the approval of God. On that day, I realized I can't please everyone. But I can please God. The same is true for you. Why work so hard to be normal, when God created you to stand out?

Part Four

Chapter 10

AN AFFAIR TO REMEMBER

My attitude toward men who mess around is simple: If you find 'em, kill 'em.

— Loretta Lynn

Consider all the planning that goes into a perfect wedding: the date, the location, the budget and guest list, the flowers, cake, music, food, and of course, most important, *the* dress. (Did you know there's a reality show on cable, called *Say Yes to the Dress*, devoted entirely to watching a variety of women shop for their wedding dress? That's the whole show, honest! Don't ask me how I know this.) While there are a few variables you can't control — the weather, people's moods and expectations, the ring bearer's attention span — most people certainly try to control as many details as possible to create an unforgettable occasion.

If you're married, you can remember specific, vivid details (I hope!) of your own special day. I recall trying to smile politely at all the people in the receiving line and move them along as quickly as possible so we could get the heck out of Dodge and start the honeymoon! Even if you're not married, chances are that you've at least thought about it: imagining how it would all look and feel, thinking about where it might be, who would be there, and of course what you'd be wearing. Most of the time, when a couple has a wedding, they plan and plan and plan. And then plan some more.

And the decisions about wedding details are just the start. The whole time leading up to your wedding, you think about and discuss where you'll live, whether you're willing to move for career advancement, whether you'd like to have children, how many, and how soon. (I wanted two, Amy wanted two, and our parents wanted us to have two, so we added those together and had six.) However, one of the biggest, most important decisions a couple can make often goes unaddressed: whether to commit adultery.

According to the Journal of Psychology and Christianity, up to 65 percent of husbands and 55 percent of wives will commit adultery by the age of forty.

Consider it for yourself — have you already planned to have an affair? Maybe in between your promotion at work but not before your fifth anniversary? Most normal people would say, "No, of course not!" Yet every day normal people end up doing hurtful things they never planned to do.

If you're a Christian, you've probably at least heard, "You shall not commit adultery." (It's one of the Ten Commandments, found in Exodus

20:14.) In the church, we consider that kind of a big one. Whether or not you've ever heard that commandment, most of us don't go into marriage anticipating — let alone planning — that one day we're going to cheat on our spouse. And yet, according to the *Journal of Psychology and Christianity*, up to 65 percent of husbands and 55 percent of wives will commit adultery by the age of forty. You don't have to be a psychologist or a Christian to know that's a lot.

HOW DO YOU GET THERE FROM HERE?

So if no one plans on committing adultery, why is it that so many people find themselves entwined with someone other than their spouse? Simple: we have a spiritual enemy whose only mission is to steal, kill, and destroy everything that matters to God. Unquestionably, God holds the covenant of marriage as a sacred bond for his children. Therefore it's a no-brainer that our enemy wants to lure as many of us as possible into adulterous sin. One of his greatest tricks — one of the first lessons in Adultery 101 — is to convince us, "That'll never happen to me." Rarely do people wake up one morning and decide they're finally going to have that affair they've been putting off. Instead, our enemy has us take baby steps toward such a destination, all the while telling ourselves, "I'd never do anything like that!"

The distance between New York City and Los Angeles is over 2,400 miles (3,900 km). Since it takes the average person two thousand steps to walk one mile, to cover the distance between the Big Apple and LA, you'd have to take almost five million steps! How could anyone do that? How in the world do you cover such an enormous distance with so many steps? You just put one foot in front of the other, one step at a time. The path from here to adultery works the same way. Your journey begins with just one single, small, seemingly innocent, subtly seductive step — followed by another, then another. You're in California before you know it.

Let's say you're watching a little TV. No big deal, just vegging after a long day, maybe channel surfing until you land on a popular show — maybe *Sex in the City, Desperate Housewives, Grey's Anatomy,* or *Two and a Half Men,* whatever. And maybe someone in this particular episode is glorifying extramarital sex. (Imagine that!) You ask yourself, "Is it really such a big deal to watch this? It's a top-ten show; everybody watches it. I mean, is it really *that* bad to watch this? I'm a smart, mature adult with good Christian values and a strong marriage. It's just a silly show. Where's the harm?"

Step one.

Maybe then one day you're thinking about the conversation you had with your spouse the night before and you realize how disappointed you were with their response. The more you think about it, the more you realize that your spouse really isn't all you'd hoped for in a soul mate. If only he understood you more and paid attention to what you really need from him. If only she listened and focused on you the way she does with the kids. You become just a little bit more dissatisfied than you were the day before. Is it really a sin to be honest about who you are and what you want? Of course not. If it's the truth, if it's how you really feel, how can it be wrong? Don't you deserve to be happy in your marriage?

A few more steps.

Maybe then you happen to meet someone who's really fun — you know, that new temp down the hall at work, the friendly new neighbor across the street, the committee chair you're working with on the fundraiser. They make you laugh a little, make you feel a little more attractive than you usually do, make you look forward to the next time you get to see them. There's nothing wrong with liking someone, is there? It's not a sin to enjoy someone's company, for heaven's sake.

Then you find yourself thinking about what a nice smile they have, how cute (maybe even a little sexy) they always look, how smart and funny and attentive they are. You really enjoy talking with them and learning more about them and how they think. You start anticipating more and more the next time you'll see them. That's normal, right? It's not a sin to look forward to talking to someone.

Only you've taken a few more steps.

Little steps add up. And they add up quickly, with one leading to several quick small steps afterward, like one domino toppling a half dozen others. Then eventually, after there's more distance between where you started and where you find yourself, you approach a line, a line you never planned to cross. One you never imagined possible. We rationalize each one so much that we lose track of when, where, or even how we crossed that line.

"Come on, Craig," you may be thinking. "Most of us have these kinds of moments — watching TV, talking with a friend at work, flirting a little with a neighbor. It's no big deal. It's normal. We all live this way." You're right, it's perfectly normal: 65 percent of husbands will cheat on their wives; at least 55 percent of wives will become emotionally and sexually involved with someone other than their husbands. Yep, totally normal. But as we've discussed, normal doesn't work. We're going to have to do something different, become weirder than normal, if we want to uphold the vows we made to someone we love very much.

ONE SMALL STEP FOR MAN . . .

"I never thought it would happen to me." I've heard these words dozens and dozens of times from so many normal people who suddenly find themselves — or more likely get found out — in the middle of a messy affair. It happened again just recently. My old high school buddy — I'll call him Tyler — sat in my office sobbing earnestly. After fourteen years of marriage and three kids ranging in age from four to eleven, Tyler had let down his guard and walked into a devastating trap.

Through the tears, he explained how it happened. As an up-and-coming manager in a tech company, Tyler was promoted twice in a five-year period. Clearly on a fast track, he poured more and more time and energy into his work. Sixty- to seventy-hour workweeks became the norm, not the exception. His wife, Lori, frequently asked him to cut back and spend more time with her and the kids, and he really intended to, but it never happened.

He and Lori used to pray together daily. But there simply wasn't time for it once Tyler began leaving earlier to jump-start his day at work. More weeks stretched between their usual date nights, until they rarely had any time alone. Early in their marriage, they committed to an annual week-end trip alone to plan their upcoming year. But there simply was never a good time to get away. And Tyler was so tired at the end of another long workday — he really just wanted to grab dinner and fall asleep in front of *SportsCenter*. Lori was never awake in the mornings now that he was getting up so early to leave for work. Soon there was no physical intimacy between them anymore.

Tyler explained that he really did love his wife. He had never imagined cheating on her or thought of himself as that kind of guy. But when his assistant at work began paying more and more attention to him, she awakened something in him that he'd forgotten was there — a need to feel appreciated and respected, a need to feel desired and comforted, a need to be vulnerable and intimate.

Most married people neglect their marriage. We don't intend to take our spouse for granted, but in reality it's easy to do. It just happens over time, a few steps here, a few steps there, all in a direction that gradually leads us farther away from home. You get busy. Distracted. Overwhelmed with work and kids, school and church, bills and chores. Tired. Exhausted even. There's no time to take care of yourself like you once did. You let yourself go a little — a few more pounds, a little less concern about what you wear or how you look. You don't necessarily give your best all the time. You're approaching a line.

Gradually you start giving more time and energy outside your marriage: to your business, to a second job, to a hobby — even to your children. Not bad things, any of them. But this busyness begins to affect your intimacy. Not just your sexual intimacy but also simply the intertwined connection you have — talking, sharing, relating, planning, dreaming, praying, laughing. You have less time to spend together, less time to talk, and less energy. You end up talking about only the necessary things, the details and decisions that don't really even matter, because it's too hard to have a real conversation about the most important things. You stop sharing what's on your heart. More and more often you're thinking about something — or someone — else anyway, so it's harder for you to be present and truly listen.

Without realizing it or acknowledging it to each other, you essentially become roommates. Neither of you intended it, but it's where you find yourselves. As you slowly drift away from each other, sexual intimacy withers. You may not have sex at all anymore — and may not even miss it, since this part of your relationship became boring and predictable.

Outside the bedroom, your thoughts wander a little. Your eyes begin to linger a little longer in places where they shouldn't. Porn used to be more of a guy problem. Statistically, though, over a third of porn users today are women. Of course, porn is available virtually everywhere in our skin-saturated culture: internet (websites, blogs, cyberchat, webcam, online hookup sites), movies (TV, cable, on-demand, theaters), television (dramas, reality shows, sitcoms), men's magazines, fashion magazines, sensually explicit novels in every genre. It becomes normal for your mind to objectify the opposite sex, to project unrealistic expectations onto your spouse, and to expect the impossible from them.

Then when someone new and attractive and interesting comes along, it's so easy to refocus your attention. Before you know it, you've formed an emotional bond with them, without even trying or wanting to. Before you know it, New York is a dim memory and you find yourself in Los Angeles.

WHATEVER IT TAKES

In Proverbs 5:8 – 11, Solomon warns his son about the dangers of the adulterous woman: "Stay away from her! Don't go near the door of her house! If you do, you will lose your honor and will lose to merciless people all you have achieved. Strangers will consume your wealth, and someone else will enjoy the fruit of your labor. In the end you will groan in anguish when disease consumes your body"

You can't build a foundation of sin now for a life of purity later.

(NLT). Solomon's simple advice here contains great wisdom: "Do *whatever it takes* to avoid temptation." Don't even get close. Don't flirt with disaster. Don't pretend like everything's okay. Do whatever it takes. Be as different, as radical, as weird as necessary to minimize (no one can eliminate it entirely) the risk.

Many people believe that they're far away from the line where the sin of physical adultery happens. They think that if they haven't already touched, kissed, or been naked together, it doesn't count. However, from God's vantage point, our sin doesn't start as soon as there's physical contact; it begins when we take any first step. Jesus makes it clear: "I tell you that anyone who *looks at a woman lustfully* has already committed adultery with her *in his heart*" (Matt. 5:28, emphasis mine). He reveals where the problem begins, and emphasizes that the seeds of seduction are just as sinfully lethal as its poison fruit. Therefore Solomon's advice is both foundational as well as practical: just stay as far away from temptation as you can. If the seed doesn't get planted, it can't become a toxic thornbush. We must guard our minds and our hearts, starting with our eyes.

If you're single, maybe you think I'm giving you a free pass. You should know me better than that by now! And it's not my standards we're talking about but God's. The vast majority of people today cross the line of sexual sin long before they're married. I call it *premarital adultery* because when you commit sexual sin today, you're cheating on the person you're going to marry later. By choosing to live outside of God's standards today, you're conditioning yourself to be even more susceptible to failure later.

You can't build a foundation of sin now for a life of purity later.

THE REWARDS OF RISK MANAGEMENT

The best way — not to mention the simplest — for singles or couples to avoid taking those first steps is to nurture and cultivate your relationship with Christ. If you stay in God's Word, if you allow his Spirit to lead you, if you live in community with other believers, then even when you begin to take steps in the wrong direction, God will immediately protect you with feelings of conviction. Distinct from feelings of guilt or shame, a sense of conviction provides us with an early warning system, a kind of "Spidey sense" of purity. If your relationship with God is truly healthy and fruitful, you'll either immediately remove yourself from the dangerous opportunity to sin or stop and turn back to him the instant you recognize you're walking into a trap. On the other hand, when you put Christ aside, when you neglect your relationship with God, you'll open up a box of kryptonite and find yourself immobilized before you even realize what happened.

DRINK FROM YOUR OWN FOUNTAIN

So how do you remain strong enough to resist sexual temptation? Fortunately, we don't have to rely on superpowers, since our friend Solomon offers us more than just a warning about what we shouldn't do. He provides a number of proactive suggestions, drawn from his wisdom, as well. In Proverbs 5:18 – 20, he encourages his son to invest passionately in his marriage: "Let your wife be a fountain of blessing for you. Rejoice in the wife of your youth. She is a loving deer, a graceful doe. Let her breasts satisfy you always. May you always be captivated by her love. Why be captivated, my son, by an immoral woman, or fondle the breasts of a promiscuous woman?" (NLT).

Want to know my paraphrase? When the grass starts to look greener somewhere else, water your own yard! Invest in your marriage with the same excitement, energy, and enthusiasm that you felt when you first met your spouse, or that you'd invest in a new relationship with someone who captured your interest. In fact, *capture* is a good word to use, because the Hebrew word that we translate as "captivated" in Solomon's advice to his son is *shagah* ("shuh-GAW").

When the grass starts to look greener somewhere else, water your own yard!

As in many cultures and their languages, in Hebrew a single word often carries an entire concept, big idea, or paradigm. *Shagah* packs this kind of passionate punch. When used literally, it conveys the energy of a wild animal pursuing, capturing, killing, and eating its prey. *Shagah* conveys a word picture of ferocious power unleashed to ravish another. Have you ever seen a lion ravish an impala? In the same way, we should be captivated, enraptured, intoxicated, utterly consumed with our spouse. Why waste that on someone else?

ACCIDENTALLY ON PURPOSE

Unfortunately, you will wind up wasting your most passionate energy on someone else if you don't deliberately channel it toward your spouse. Think about it. Have you ever accidentally slammed your finger in a door? Or accidentally gotten lost? Or how about sending a text to the wrong person by mistake? We experience unplanned missteps all the time, often through carelessness, impatience, recklessness, or distraction. Understandable, then, how so many normal people "accidentally" slide into an adulterous relationship.

While some accidents can be prevented or controlled, we rarely count on them to achieve our desired result. You don't hope to accidentally send an old friend the

> **Great marriages never happen by accident. They always happen on purpose.**

wrong email just so you can reconnect. No, you write them deliberately and let them know you're thinking of them and want to catch up. Similarly, I don't know anyone who ever accidentally ended up with a great marriage. Great marriages never happen by accident. They always happen on purpose. Here are five (not-so-easy) ways to focus your *shagah* exclusively on your spouse and together build the marriage you've always wanted.

1. *Get transparent.* Open up. Share your feelings and what's going on inside of you. Transparency comes naturally for many people, including my wife, Amy. Honestly, many days I struggle with knowing, expressing, and sharing what I'm feeling. If you share my struggle, keep in mind that your spouse will be your best teacher if you're humble enough. Amy often has to remind me, "I understand what you're thinking, but what are you *feeling*? Share

your emotions, not just your thoughts." Great communication is essential in a strong marriage — particularly at an emotional level.

2. *Get alone.* Take time by yourself to think about, pray about, and reflect on where your marriage is and where you both want it to be. Then get alone with each other. Lock doors, get sitters, plan getaways, and go on real dates — not just a movie and fast food. Remember how you fell in love in the first place? You made time alone with each other. It's basic, but we tend to overlook it.

3. *Get spiritual.* Don't overcomplicate this. Pray, read God's Word, and get together regularly with other believers. Get it on your schedule and make it sacred. One of the greatest contributors to the strength of my and Amy's marriage has been our commitment to the small group that meets in our home. We started meeting several years ago as four Christian couples eager to grow by sharing our lives together. As our trust and accountability have grown, we have been able to confront, challenge, and encourage one another in amazing ways, particularly regarding our marriages.

4. *Get help.* If you'll be honest, you know whether you've already been taking the steps we've been talking about. If you have, don't put off getting help anymore. Make an appointment — this week — with a Christian counselor. Talk to your pastor. Or talk to a trusted friend or mentor. Don't settle for mediocrity in your marriage by being a coward. Take radical action. Look your struggles in the eye and acknowledge the truth about them, about your spouse, about yourself.

5. *Get naked.* Can I get an amen? This one doesn't require any explanation. I already said it before: Water your own yard. Invest passionately in your marriage.

LOVE NEVER FAILS

God's timing never ceases to amaze me. As I was researching statistics, preparing to write this chapter, my phone rang. It was a guy who sometimes attends our church. In between sobs, he managed to get out, "Craig, I've been committing adultery. But I got caught. And I just now told my wife." The fact that I had recently been interviewing people about recovery placed me in a unique position to connect him with just the right people.

Later that week I went to check up on him. I asked him how he was holding up, and he said, "Without a doubt, this has been the worst week of my entire life. But at the same time, I think it's also been the best week of my life."

I said, "Um, I'm going to need you to explain that."

He said, "Well, for years I've been learning about God, talking about him, and thinking about him. But I've never really *known* him. But I've just been so broken. Now I think, for the first time ever, I actually know him."

At that moment, I realized there was more hope for his marriage than ever before — because Christ had finally become a very real part of their equation. I don't advocate divorce. The Bible makes it clear: God hates divorce (Mal. 2:16). When a person commits adultery, there are biblical grounds for divorce. But don't ever forget: adultery is also biblical grounds for forgiveness, healing, and restoration. What God makes new is often so much better than anything you ever imagined before. No matter what sin you find yourself in, turn to God. Let him forgive, heal, and

When a person commits adultery, there are biblical grounds for divorce. But don't ever forget: adultery is also biblical grounds for forgiveness.

restore. Psalm 51:17 says, "The sacrifices of God are a broken spirit; a broken and contrite heart, O God, you will not despise." When you reach out to God humbly, you'll find that he's already reaching out to you.

If you've been on that path toward adultery, or if you're already there, ask God to do what only he can do. Ask him to strengthen you with his Spirit as you sever that flirty relationship at work that's teetering on the edge or as you put a porn filter on your computer or talk honestly with your spouse about what you've been seeing. You should acknowledge the truth that every step toward adultery causes so many strong emotions: hurt and guilt, betrayal and shame, anger and fear, bitterness and worry. You may need to see a counselor, a trusted mature couple with a strong marriage, or your pastor. Do not resist getting the resources you need to do whatever it takes to get your marriage back on track.

> "If you think you are standing firm, be careful that you don't fall!"

Trust God to work with you on a day-by-day basis. Ask him to replace the spectrum of painful emotions in your marriage with one of healing and hope, renewal and comfort, forgiveness and faith, restoration and peace. Romans 5:20 reminds us that "where sin increased, grace increased all the more." Ask God to bring all the secret things to light once and for all so you can deal with them honestly. It would not be difficult for you to imagine the destruction your sin could cause in your life and in the lives of those you care about. Instead imagine what it might be like to have a life of purity, without secrets, without lies. What would that feel like? How free that would be! With God's grace and mercy, that place is within your reach.

If you haven't committed adultery, even in your heart, that's great, but I still want to caution you. In 1 Corinthians 10:12 – 13, Paul says, "If you think you are standing firm, be careful that you don't fall! No temptation has seized you except what is common to man. And God is faithful; he will not let you be tempted beyond what you can bear. But when you are tempted, he will also provide a way out so that you can stand up under it." Watch out. The instant you sense that your next step might be a seductive one leading toward adultery, reconsider. God promises you a way out. Find that way out, and take it.

No one sets out a plan with the express goal of having an affair. However, having an affair has become the norm for the majority of people. They take a few steps at a time until they find themselves at a destination they never intended to reach. Weird people watch their steps each day and work backward from the possibility of an affair to how they can protect themselves and their marriage. Weird people love well.

Chapter 11

SEX CYMBALS

Love is the answer, but while you are waiting for the answer sex raises some pretty good questions.

— WOODY ALLEN

ave you seen the old *I Love Lucy* episodes where Lucy and Ricky sleep in separate twin beds? Even though their characters were married on the show, and the actors were married to each other in *real life*, network censors insisted that the Ricardos' bedroom scenes remain as chaste and nonsuggestive as possible. The line between reality and Lucy's TV world blurred once again when both actor and character became pregnant with her first child. On the show, however, the word *pregnant* was considered sexually explicit and therefore could not be used. Euphemisms like *expecting* and *with child* were used instead.

Considering what airs today (and I'm talking network TV, not cable or adult access), it's clear we've come a long way, baby. "The subject of sex has been part of the medium almost since its start. But displays of sex, intimacy and even body parts, for the most part, have been evolutionary, not revolutionary," writes journalist Gary Strauss in a recent article for *USA Today*.[6] We have shows depicting suggestive acts, trivializing perverted practices, and tossing off double entendres as if everything in the world relates back to sex. And maybe it does.

We live in a sexually saturated culture — explicit images assault us 24/7, anonymous cyber encounters lure us, and online businesses cater to every fetish imaginable (and some I hope we can't imagine!). In contrast to the beautiful music that God intends between a husband and wife, now we hear countless sex cymbals clanging in our ears. "If I speak in the tongues of men and of angels, but have not love, I am only a resounding gong or a clanging cymbal" (1 Cor. 13:1). Loveless and lust-based, sex cymbals promise instant gratification and fulfillment of our every fantasy but ultimately leave us empty and broken. If we don't guard against them, our culture's seductive siren will drown out the sound of God's voice.

LOUD AND CLEAR

No other area in our culture today has a more toxic, crippling effect on who God wants us to be and how he made us as men and women than sex. If we want to be healthy, whole, and holy, we must make conscious, deliberate choices to keep our hearts pure and our bodies sacred. We must be willing to be even weirder than usual. We must tune our hearts to our Master's voice so we hear him above the clamor.

Otherwise we'll live reactively and find ourselves traveling down a path guaranteed to get us lost in the wilderness. Not only do temptations related to sex assault us every day, but they carry with them major life-changing consequences. Apparently, though, we rarely take the consequences seriously enough. Honestly, when was the last time you heard someone say,

> "This year, I'm finally starting that affair I've been talking about."
> "Porn is so much more emotionally satisfying than any human relationship."
> "You know, I've always wanted an STD. Do you know anyone who's infected? Do you think they'd have sex with me?"
> "I wonder what would happen if I had sex with my coworker today. Surely they wouldn't fire me, would they? I've gotta try that."

Forgive me if these sound flippant, but I don't know a single person who actually thinks like this, and yet I know hundreds of people who've fallen into these very circumstances by their poor choices in weak moments. Once again, it's become the norm.

In our previous chapter, we talked about how the specific sin of adultery blooms when people take just a few small steps in the wrong direction. We should keep in mind, however, that these steps don't always lead to adultery; they can evolve into a variety of life-choking, soul-deadening sexual sins: porn addictions, promiscuity, prostitution, homosexuality, and other perversions. Like a trap waiting for a wild animal to walk blindly toward it, sexual sin imprisons every area of your life — emotional, physical, psychological, and spiritual.

Which brings us back to the foundational problem: the reason people fall into *any* sexual sin is because they get too close to the opportunities. People who get too close lack what I call a moral margin. If the best way to avoid adultery is to stay off the path that leads there,

The reason people fall into *any* sexual sin is because they get too close to the opportunities.

then having a moral margin to fend off all areas of sexual immorality requires building a buffer, a wall between yourself and the opportunities for sexual sin. Then digging a moat around that wall. Then flooding that moat. Then filling the moat with electric eels and alligators. Then putting razor wire on top of the wall. Then ... well, you get the idea.

SPRINT FOR PURITY

You might wonder why we're spending so much time talking about sexual temptation and how to combat it. Of course, many other normal things can tempt us and turn us away from God. However, the apostle Paul gives this topic special attention because it has the potential to be one of the most dangerous and devastating. To emphasize his message, Paul practically uses the equivalent of a text in all caps. In 1 Corinthians 6:18, he shouts, "Flee from sexual immorality." He doesn't say "flirt." He doesn't say "flaunt." He yells, "Flee!" — which, translated from the Greek word *pheugo* ("FYOO-goh"), literally means to run away, to shun, to distance oneself, to escape danger. It's an urgent verb that forces you to take notice: *pheugo* from sexual immorality! Go — stop hesitating! Get out of harm's way — now! Put some distance between you and temptation! Run, Forrest, run!

The Bible doesn't tell us to flee from overeating, from gossip, from lying, or from any other category of sin. It says to flee — right now! — from sexual immorality. Normal people ask, "How close can I get without going too far?" I'll answer with some questions. "How close can you get to a rattlesnake without it being dangerous? How long can you hold a live electrical wire without getting electrocuted?" Wise people put as much distance between themselves and sexual temptation as possible. They not only get away but also plan their escape route.

Certainly, we should resist all areas in which we're tempted. But all sins are not the same from God's point of view. The consequences vary, depending on the severity of the sin. Speeding, telling a white lie, and committing adultery are all sins. But the consequences vary. Sinning sexually often carries a higher cost.

For example, sexual sin can cost you your marriage. It might jeopardize custody of your kids. It will steal your self-esteem and trash your reputation. It could cost your job. Ultimately, if you contract a sexual disease, it could even cost you your life. One bad decision sexually can literally cost you for the rest of your life.

THIS IS MY BODY

Paul explains why sexual sin carries such severe consequences: "All other sins a man commits are outside his body, but he who sins sexually sins against his own body. Do you not know that your body is a temple of the Holy Spirit, who is in you, whom you have received from God? You are not your own; you were bought at a price. Therefore honor God with your body" (1 Cor. 6:18–20). Clearly, sexual sin is different because its consequences stick with you. The collateral damage of sexual impurity is painful, emotional, and deeply spiritual.

It's common in our culture for people to say, "This is my body. I can do whatever I want with it." Actually, if you're a believer in Christ, according to the verse we just read, this is not true. You're now a house for God, a dwelling place for his Spirit. When we sin sexually, we erode the very foundation of who God created us to be as men and women.

In case we've missed his point elsewhere, Paul gets even more specific in Ephesians 5:3: "Among you there must not be even a *hint* of sexual immorality" (emphasis mine). Think about this phrase: *not even a hint.* We tend to compare ourselves with those around us. "Hey, I'm better than most people." The problem is that the world's standards are so much lower than God's. We think, "At least I'm not doing [fill in the blank with some terrible thing] like that other person is doing." But God says, "not even a *hint* of sexual immorality."

Call me old-fashioned if you like (and yes, with six kids I'm feeling older every day), but God makes it clear that anything we sexualize can trip us up. The phrase we translate as "sexual immorality" comes from the Greek word *porneia* ("pohr-NAY-uh"). Which should sound familiar — it's the basis for our word *pornography*, which we've shortened to *porn*. *Porneia* literally means anything that causes sexual arousal outside of marriage. Yep, that's right — *anything*.

PORN AGAIN

Like most of us, I grew up with intense curiosity about the opposite sex. Other than a clandestine quest to see my sister's Barbie naked and a few peeks at naked pygmies in *National Geographic*, my childhood naïveté remained intact until I was ten — when my first exposure to actual porn shattered it. My friend Stephen, also ten, had discovered his dad's hidden stash of *Playboy* magazines. He beamed like he'd just found buried treasure when he boasted of his discovery to me. Together we inspected those glossy pages in total awe.

I don't know what it is like to do drugs, but the high must be similar to the hormone-charged, adrenaline-fueled rush I got staring at those pictures for the first time. I still remember the airbrushed images vividly — as if they were forever burned onto the hard drive of my brain. I may not recall a single thing I learned in high school algebra, but I can retrieve Miss February's image in an instant.

Sadly, this is the norm. According to a 2002 survey from the London School of Economics, nine out of ten children between ages eight to sixteen have viewed pornography online. Ninety percent! It's tragic that seeing porn is totally normal for kids nowadays. According to the survey, in most cases the children reported that they saw something accidentally, often while doing homework and using a search engine with a word that seemed innocent enough.

Such early exposure to porn by the vast majority may help explain why porn viewing and porn addictions have risen dramatically for women. For decades, we've tended to think that porn is a man-only problem, with little to no usage by women. Today, however, over a third of adult websites are visited by women.[7] While it's generally accepted that women are wired differently than men — being aroused more by connectedness than by visual stimulation — studies find that once women have been exposed to pornography, they can just as easily become addicted.

JUST A TASTE

The impact of viewing porn reminds me of a story I heard about how Eskimos used to deal with wolves that attacked their livestock. (Warning: the story I'm about to tell you is disgusting and may gross you out!) Eskimo villagers would kill a rabbit or some other small game and then drain its blood. They'd dip a razor-sharp, double-edged knife into the blood and freeze it. By repeating this process numerous times, they would freeze layer upon layer of the animal blood around the deadly blade — making essentially a blood popsicle on a knife. (Are you grossed out yet?)

Then the villagers would take the knife to the outskirts of their settlement, where the wolves had been active, and secure the blade to stick straight up from the ground. During the night, when a wolf would come and smell the blood, he'd start licking. And licking. And licking. As the wolf would lick away on the bloodsicle, his tongue would become numb. He'd keep licking, gradually working his way through the blood, all the way down to the blade. But by this time, because his tongue was so numb from the cold, he wouldn't feel it as the blade started slashing his tongue. In fact, the taste of his own warm blood would excite him, causing him to lick even faster. By the time the wolf would figure out what was happening, it was too late. His tongue shredded and bleeding profusely, he'd wander off somewhere and bleed to death. (Told you it was gross.)

This is how pornography works. It starts with just a taste, just a glance. Gradually it begins to numb your senses. It's exciting, seductive, enticing. It feels so good. In the rush of the moment, you continue using it, coming back to it again and again, not realizing that you're wounding yourself. By the time you realize how wounded you are, it's usually too late.

SOME BRICKS FOR YOUR WALL

Clearly, we must fortify our moral margin if we are to resist the snares of porn and other sexual enticements. How do we create a wall strong enough to protect our hearts from the assault of deadly temptations? Here are eight principles to use as building blocks in constructing a barrier between yourself and sexual sin. Many are aimed at single people, although they apply to everyone. Married people simply need to build their walls and give the only key to their spouse.

You know these principles will be weird, but keep in mind that we want results that are weird as well. We don't want to be normal, especially when it comes to how most people handle sexual temptations and opportunities for immorality. Weird makes you truly sexy in a way the world can never know.

1. Dress for spiritual success. Dress in a way that brings glory to God. Put simply, "Be modest." This applies equally to women and men.

Romans 14:13 says, "Decide ... to live in such a way that you will not cause another believer to stumble and fall." Why would you entice those around you to sin? Ladies, I know you may have paid a lot of money for those skimpy clothes, but save them for your husband, whether you're currently married or not. Guys, I know you spent months in the gym to develop that muscle-stud body, but don't display it with skintight clothes. Think about how you want to represent Christ as you interact with other people. Dress for spiritual success.

2. Keep four feet on the floor. If you're dating, both of you keep your feet on the floor when you're together. It's amazing how complicated it can be to get naughty when all four feet are on the floor. Don't sit on the bed to do your Bible study together. (You're not fooling anybody, you know.) Don't wrap your legs around each other. If you're watching a movie together, keep all your feet on the floor.

Maybe this sounds silly to you, but it's a proven scientific fact: when smooth-shaved legs rub against hairy legs, clothing vanishes. It happens and you know it. The solution isn't rocket science. Keep four feet on the floor.

3. No playing house, and no sleepovers. Nowadays it's very normal for people who are seriously dating to wind up sharing toothbrushes. It happens so naturally. You're together late. Everything's innocent. The movie or concert or church trip or whatever ends late. You're both sleepy.

"Don't go — it's such a long drive." (Whether it's two miles or two hundred, it's always "such a long drive.")

"You can just sleep on the couch." (Conveniently located in your bedroom.)

"Here, you can wear my T-shirt. Let's just cuddle!" (Translation: "Let's get ready to make out and blame it on the late hour.")

In every instance, you're basically saying, "Hey, I know! Let's see if this rattlesnake bites." Don't play games. Don't play house. If you're not married, then wait to have sleepovers.

4. *No tonsil hockey.* Don't make out. Granted, this is my rule and my gift to you, not the eleventh commandment. If you try to draw your line as close to the edge as possible ("I want us to explore our relationship, but we can't have sex"), then the line won't hold. Instead of a rock fortress, you'll have a few pieces of cardboard taped together. If you want real safety, real purity, and real respect for the other person, you'll build a real wall. You'll find distance between you and temptation. Which means you'll put distance between you and sin. Don't make out. It's just not worth the risk.

When Amy and I were dating, we laid out clear rules. We were absolutely committed that we would wait until we were married to share the gift of lovemaking. And we were never even tempted. Not once. Until we kissed, that is. When we did kiss for the first time, temperatures rose, fireworks exploded, angels sang. Just having her face close to mine, body close to body — it was too much. This is when temptation started.

Is it extreme not to kiss? Weird not to make out? Sure. But if you want different results, you have to do something different.

5. *Avoid dangerous places.* What are dangerous places? They're different for different people. What places create temptation for you? Is it going to a bar with people after work? Chat rooms? Facebook? The gym? Then don't go to those places. Buy *P90X* or *Abs of Steel* or Jillian's *30 Day Shred* — and stay at home. Go to a friend's house instead of the bars. When you see danger, flee. Avoid it. Cross the street. What's dangerous for you? Figure out what your alternatives are, and avoid the risk. Going closer to the fire you know will ignite you is foolish.

6. *Avoid time alone with the wrong people.* Who's risky for you? Who tempts you? It may not even be somebody you're attracted to. It could be just a friend who always manages to lead you into compromising trouble. Get away from that person. Here's some free advice: a friend who leads you toward trouble is not a friend. Ditch them. Get yourself some godly friends who will build you up, lift you up, and help you live the life of honesty and holiness that you want. Real friends will help strengthen your moral margin, not knock it down.

And if you are dating someone who is distracting you from God, why are you wasting your time? Dump him or her. Why settle for a fixer-upper when God wants you to have his best?

7. *Guard your eyes, your mind, and your heart.* Remember, your body belongs to Christ. Honor him with your body. Watch out for every hint of sexual immorality. You want to talk about extreme? Don't check your mailbox. I'm serious. If the Victoria's Secret "catalog" comes to your house, first of all, why? What about *Sports Illustrated*? Maybe you've heard of a little thing called the swimsuit issue. What about *GQ*? How many scantily clad women (and men) are lurking between those covers? Why are you allowing temptation like that into your home? *Subscribing* to it? *Asking* for it to be delivered right inside your castle gates? Even *paying* for it? Are you crazy? It's a Trojan horse and you know it.

8. *If computer porn is a problem, have your internet monitored.*
Many products are available for you to install on your computer (or your phone) to keep you honest. While I don't endorse any specific product, I use Covenant Eyes. Every click I make is recorded, scored, and reported to two of my close friends — who also just happen to be on the board of directors of our church. If I click on anything even marginally questionable, I have some explaining to do.

Do you like romance novels? Watch soap operas? Telenovelas on Telemundo? Be careful what you're putting before your eyes, feeding into your imagination. You know how if you feed a stray, it's really hard to get rid of it? Temptation is like that. And just as with a stray, you know how you can make it go away? Don't feed it. Put up a fence around your yard. Build your wall. At every opportunity ask yourself, "Is what I'm doing, is what I'm looking at, is what I'm thinking, honoring God? Is it honoring my spouse?" If you're not married, is it honoring your future spouse?

If this all sounds like a radical lifestyle change, then you've finally got it. We have to consider everything, not just magazines and books. Television. Movies. Music. The kinds of conversations you get yourself into. What are you thinking about? What you are fantasizing about? What memories are you lingering on? Take those thoughts captive. Make them obedient to Christ (2 Cor. 10:5).

All of these safeguards may seem really extreme. And they are. *Fleeing* is extreme behavior. If we weren't meant to be extreme, Paul would have used a different word: "Casually stroll away" from sexual immorality or "take your time and crawl away" from it. But he doesn't, does he?

Instead, he yells, "Get out of there! Make a break!" He shouts with the urgency of a firefighter revealing the exit to a person trapped in a burning building. So many people have fallen prey to sexual temptation, to sexual sin. We lie to ourselves that it won't happen to us, even when we know the statistics, even when we know our odds ... even when we know ourselves.

YOU'RE FREE TO GO NOW

We've now reconsidered the reality of what exists all around us today, explored the truth of what God's Word has to say about sexual immorality, and developed practical, sensible strategies that can help you create and reinforce a moral margin. These strategies represent the things that you can do to set the stage for what only God can do. In the culture we live in today, virtually no one walks around without some sexual wounds. Your mind is injured, your soul is numb. While you can protect your injury and prevent it from getting worse, remember that only God can heal it. And he wants to.

How can you keep yourself open to God's presence in the area of your sexuality? Ask him to forgive you and to heal you. Then tell the person (or the people) who need to hear it, and ask for their forgiveness, or for help, or for both. Don't give in to the lie that there must be some other way, that you can figure out something else. If you could do this yourself, then why haven't you? You would have if you could. But you can't.

If you've been trapped by pornography, it's time to deal with it. Face it and see it for what it is: somewhere along the way, you got injured. It's time to get healed. It's time to confess. Falling for the bait doesn't make you the worst person in the world. You were snared. You were hooked. But you don't have to stay that way.

Now is the time to deal with the shackles that keep you enslaved. Today you can leave the prison that sexual immorality has created from your past mistakes. Hear your Father's voice call out to you above the noisy clamor of our culture. He says, "I love you. You're free to go now. Sexual sin has no hold on you."

He upholds the cause of the oppressed
*   and gives food to the hungry.*
The LORD sets prisoners free,
*   the LORD gives sight to the blind,*
the LORD lifts up those who are bowed down,
*   the LORD loves the righteous.*

— Psalm 146:7 – 8

Chapter 12

A DIFFERENT KIND OF EDUCATION

Sex education may be a good idea in the schools, but I don't believe the kids should be given homework.

— BILL COSBY

A dad came home from work and parked in the driveway. As he got out of his car, his beautiful princess, eight-year-old Brooke, came bounding out to see him.

"Daddy! Daddy!"

He smiled broadly, stooped down to her level, and swung his arms out wide. Brooke never slowed down, plowing right into his embrace. They hugged for a moment, then he stood up and took her hand, and they walked up the sidewalk together. As they strolled, Brooke looked up into his face and asked innocently, "Daddy, what is sex?"

His earth stopped spinning. His mind was reeling. Maybe his wife should be the one to have this first talk. No, he'd be strong and do the best he could. *I knew I was going to have to have this conversation someday,* he thought. *You just never think it's going to be* today. He drew in a long, deep sigh and stopped walking. Sitting on the front steps with her next to him, he began, "Okay, honey. You asked, so here it is ..."

He started with boys and girls, how they're different, how they have different feelings and different shapes. He talked about Adam and Eve. He talked about the virtues of love and courtship, and how important it is for mommies and daddies to get married when they know God wants them to. He quoted Song of Songs and Proverbs. He talked about how eggs get fertilized, about how an embryo is a real, live baby, entire and complete, and finally brought everything around full circle. He really wished he had some diagrams or a book or something, but considering how unexpected their talk was, it seemed to go well enough. Brooke just sat there, listening carefully, her bright eyes wide.

"Honey, I know that was a lot all at once. Do you have any questions?"

Brooke stammered, "Oh yeah, um, well, I don't get all that, Daddy. But I was gonna ask you before ... Mommy's in the kitchen. When you drove up, she told me to come and tell you dinner would be ready in a couple of secs. What is 'secs'?"

LAYS AND LIES

Most of us don't know how to talk to our kids about sex. It's awkward and uncomfortable, and it's hard to steer the conversation the way you want. You never know what they're going to ask or why they're asking. You want to be completely truthful, but you don't want to tell more than they're ready to hear. You want to tell them enough to inform and protect them, but not so much that you awaken their curiosity. And the last thing you want is to give them a user manual with a sense of permission. This is why it's perfectly normal for most parents to avoid this subject entirely.

Unfortunately, a variety of user manuals are already available everywhere. Most parents choose by default to allow complete strangers to inform their kids about sex and to influence how they'll behave with this new information. Through culture, through school, through television and movies, through advertising, through the internet, and especially through their friends — your kids can easily learn details about sex you've never heard of or even imagined.

It's so easy to keep it vague and friendly, open-ended as if you're just another resource, available to answer their questions as needed. But we have to remember: we're part of a war. We have a spiritual enemy who wants to steal our kids' purity and destroy as many of them as he can. Satan's all too happy to get all the details, and then some, into our kids' hands and minds. He's trying to normalize sex and neutralize the sinful consequences of disobeying God. Consider these five lies he's pushing on your kids *right now*:

1. *"Sex is no big deal — it's like eating, sleeping, breathing."* What's normal? Teen pregnancy is so 2007. Nobody gets pregnant anymore. Birth control is popular, convenient, and easy to obtain. If you manage to make it to eighteen and still have your virginity — let alone all the way to *marriage* — most of your friends won't admire you. They'll feel sorry for you — you're weird beyond belief. "Premarital sex" sounds so outdated. It's not like you expect to get married or anything. Let's call it "friends with benefits" instead.
2. *"Oral sex doesn't really count."* It's not like you're doing the ultimate deed. Even if you do "everything but . . . ," congratulations! You're still *technically* a virgin. If Bill Clinton, the forty-second president of the United States, says oral sex

doesn't count as sexual relations, then who are your parents to tell you it does?

3. *"Bisexuality is cool."* It's hip, open-minded, and a great way to double your pleasure. Being sexual with both men and women is a great way to explore. It doesn't make you gay — just curious. Curiosity is a sign of intelligence, right? So let's call this "bi-curious." How are you supposed to know what you really like if you don't order off both menus? You want to know why your parents make such a big deal about being bi-curious? It's because they're afraid of their own desires — they're uptight and repressed. Not like you and your friends.

4. *"Porn is another great way to explore your sexuality."* It's perfectly natural and saves you the trouble of having to hook up with one of your friends with benefits. Besides, sex in those films and websites is between consenting adults, so who's it hurting, really? Like we just mentioned: being curious only proves how smart — not to mention passionate — you are. Besides, how are you supposed to learn how to do everything and satisfy your partners? Do you honestly think your parents (a) actually know any of this stuff and (b) would tell you how it works if they did? (Like you'd want that anyway — gross!)

5. *"Modesty is for losers."* It's for homely, unpopular kids who don't know how to look hot — or can't afford the right clothes. Dressing hot shows self-confidence and allows you to express how hip you are. And you're never going to have a better body than you do when you're a teenager. You'll never look this good again. Don't waste that waist. It's not like your clothes are fooling anybody. Why should you try to hide how hot you are? That doesn't even make sense. It sounds hypocritical. (Besides, having "FOXY" across the butt of your sweatpants is, well ... foxy.)

These are just a few of the lies about sex that kids absorb today. Clearly, a lot of adults believe these things too. If you want your kids to be different, you're going to have to teach them what that even looks like. You need to tell them, "Here's why you can't trust what the people around you are saying: 'When [the devil] lies, he speaks his native language, for he is a liar and the father of lies'" (John 8:44). How can you tell when the devil is lying? His lips are moving. When the world tells your kids, "This is great! This is how you should be," your kids need to be able to see through those lies. First John 4:1 warns us, "Do not believe every spirit, but test the spirits to see whether they are from God." How can you teach your kids how to tell where the things they're hearing are coming from?

WHAT'S ON YOUR MIND?

Once you've identified Satan's blatant lies and the sugar coating he serves them in, it's important to contrast their taste with something truly sweet: the truth of Jesus. In John 8:32, he says, "Then you will know the truth, and the truth will set you free." Notice how it's not just the truth that sets you free — the knowing part is critical. Just acknowledging that truth exists out there somewhere isn't enough. If your children (and you, for that matter) don't know what the Scriptures say about sex, even if you accept and trust the Bible as God's inspired, authoritative Word, then it's easy to believe unbiblical messages from non-Christian sources.

Curiously enough, almost every time we talk about sex in church, many people get angry. Some even write letters: "This kind of talk does not belong in church!" My response is always, "Then where does it belong? In the locker room at school? Between the pages of *Playboy* or *Cosmo*? In the back row of the bus returning from youth camp?" If you honestly think that church is not the place to talk about sex, then I challenge you to examine your reasons.

Mind-blowing, God-honoring sex begins between your ears, not between your legs.

In order to explain biblical truth and have open, ongoing discussions with your kids about how God views our sexuality, you must embrace the foundational premise: Great Godly Sex (GGS) starts with how you think, not how you feel. Mind-blowing, God-honoring sex begins between your ears, not between your legs. Forgive me if this sounds crass, but I think we have to deal directly here. Proverbs 14:12 warns us, "There is a way that seems right to a man, but in the end it leads to death."

If you want your kids to know the truth about sex — and more specific, if you want them to know what's important about how God views sex — then you're going to have to risk being uncomfortable, embarrassed, and afraid. You must step up and tell them the truth they're so hungry to hear. Otherwise they'll accept whatever crumbs of hearsay and popular opinion fall their way. If you have kids, and they're school-age (older than six), then they're already hearing explicit details that are much, much more graphic than anything written here. Bottom line, you have to ask yourself, "Who do I want controlling this conversation with my kids?"

WHYS, NOT LIES

If you want your kids to be better than normal, you must accept the responsibility that it begins with you. You can cover the "what" of sexual immorality, but the whats are not enough by themselves. If we don't teach our kids the "why," they're going to say the same thing we wrestled with at their age: why *not*? Here are some truths you can share with your kids to combat the lies and answer their whys.

We're made to stick. The apostle Paul addressed sexuality in his first letter to the church at Corinth, and to appreciate his message fully, you need to know that Corinth was the original Sin City. As a large, easily accessible port city, Corinth became the destination of choice for the many visitors who came there wanting what happened in Corinth to stay in Corinth. Frankly, this city offered pretty much whatever kind of sex anyone could want. Some people even paid for sex as a form of worship to win the favor of a few pagan gods. Farmers commonly visited temple prostitutes in hopes that the gods would make their lands more fertile. Can't you just imagine a wheat farmer telling his wife, "Well, honey, I'll be back in a few days. I've got to visit Corinth and fertilize those crops again!"

Knowing that his audience knew Corinth and its pleasure well, Paul wasn't afraid to tell it like it is: "Do you not know that your bodies are members of Christ himself? Shall I then take the members of Christ and unite them with a prostitute? Never! Do you not know that he who unites himself with a prostitute is one with her in body? For it is said, 'The two will become one flesh'" (1 Cor. 6:15 – 16).

So what's the big deal here? To understand the true stickiness of sex, we need to go back to the beginning. God's plan for men and women being together seems straightforward right from the start: "For this reason a man will leave his father and mother and be united to his wife, and they will become one flesh. The man and his wife [Adam and Eve] were both naked, and they felt no shame" (Gen. 2:24 – 25).

When a man and his wife are united, they share in the covenant expression of lovemaking. In God's perfect plan, the virgin husband enters into the virgin woman. With his penetration, she sheds blood. (As with all sacred covenants, blood is shed.) A holy, righteous physical moment seals their spiritual covenant. They can be naked together without being ashamed, joined in sexual union as the two become one.

Sex joins two people spiritually and emotionally as well as physically. This is its purpose — to bond a couple together. Sex connects and fuses people together. It's sticky. Similarly, if you're stuck to someone and you try to pull loose, it's going to hurt. You're both going to leave pieces of yourselves behind. (Remind me to tell you a tragic story about my kids' pet hamster, Fuzzy, and his life-changing accident with one of those super-glue-strip kind of mousetraps. *Ouch.* Or the time my younger sister came screaming, "There's a dog stuck to our dog — and I can't get them apart!")

Imagine you took a length of really sticky tape, like duct tape or gorilla tape, and stuck it to your shirt. What if you pulled that off and stuck it to somebody else? What if you pulled it off again and stuck it to someone else? What if you did this ten times? Twenty? A hundred? After a certain point, no matter how hard you try, you can't get it to stick to anyone, because the tape is no longer sticky. You've left a tiny bit of whatever-makes-tape-sticky with each person you encountered.

Of course, sex is more powerful than duct tape. When you become physically intimate with another person, it bonds you. It unites you. It's sticky. Then when you end that relationship and go to another person, you've lost some of your stickiness. The more you do it, the less special it becomes. The less you have left of your heart and soul and uniqueness to give to the next person. Over time and among many partners, you're not very sticky anymore. It's harder to bond. More difficult to unite. You can't maintain a relationship. The other person doesn't feel connected to you, and you don't feel connected to anyone. Teach your kids to hold on to their stickiness for the person to whom they want to be stuck for the rest of their lives.

Sex is a huge deal. Sex is one of the most precious gifts with which we've been entrusted. We are created in God's image as male and female. As our loving Father, he has plans to bless us, not to harm us (Jer. 29:11). It wasn't good for man to be alone, so God created woman for man. He wanted the two to become one flesh, so he gave them the intimate act of lovemaking, which symbolizes the covenant relationship between them (Gen. 2:18 – 25). It's a profoundly big deal to be joined together, to stick to each other forever as one (Mark 10:5 – 9).

Everything counts. Tell your kids the truth: "Actually, oral sex is sex." According to the Bible, sexual immorality is porneia (you'll recall we looked at this term in the last chapter), which means any kind of sexual arousal outside of marriage. Your body isn't meant for porneia. It's meant for the Lord (1 Cor. 6:13). Just because you don't engage in penetration doesn't mean you don't face the consequences of sexual sin (Gal. 6:7 – 8). If it feels sexually arousing, it's sex. And if the person you're with isn't your spouse, it's sin and will mess you up.

Experimentation is always dangerous. Like lighting a match in a gunpowder factory, bisexuality or any kind of experimentation will only destroy us. Acknowledge the way our culture and media soft-sell sexual curiosity as license to try anything, but tell your kids what God says about it. Let them know that any dabbling in homosexuality is wrong. I know it's not popular or politically correct, and I know it offends some people to hear the truth, but God created man and woman for each other (Gen. 2:18 – 25). When you consider the way God made male and female bodies, homosexuality is clearly unnatural. And regardless of how it feels or what Will and Grace or Ellen and Rosie have to say, it's clear that God considers it sinful (Lev. 18:22; 20:13; Rom. 1:26 – 27; 1 Cor. 6:9 – 10). There's nothing cool about turning against God. There's nothing fun or cute or right about compromising who God created you to be.

You weren't born for porn. Don't be afraid to be loud and clear about the truth. Pornography is harmful. It's a self-centered, unnatural way to feed the lustful desires of your own flesh (Matt. 5:27 – 28). If you allow your thoughts to linger on sexual immorality, you're turning your heart toward sin — on purpose (Mark 7:20 – 22; James 1:15; Job 31:1). We're supposed to be consciously thinking about God and the things he considers most important — eternal things (Col. 3:1 – 8). To add insult to injury, porn degrades people. It presents human beings as soulless, conscience-less, moral-less objects. Pornography replaces the warmth and light of true human intimacy with the wildfire of self-first, sexual lust. Ask your kids if they've seen a field or mountainside after a wildfire has consumed it; remind them of the charred, black, lifeless remains.

Modesty is cooler than being hot. Help your kids become aware about the way our clothes, or lack thereof, convey messages — about who we are, what we're like, and what we want. Explain that when they dress immodestly, it sends a clear sexual message, whether they intend it to or not. Stress that the way they dress reflects the way they think about themselves. Remind them, "In God's eyes, you are beautiful and special. If you have to dress provocatively to get some guy (or girl), then you don't want that person. You deserve better than that" (1 Sam. 16:7; Prov. 31:30; Col. 3:12 – 14; 1 Peter 3:3 – 4).

CREATED TO STAND

If you've never thought about how to teach your kids to stay sexually pure, you might feel a little overwhelmed about now. More likely, most of us haven't wanted to go there, to face the reality that our precious baby girl or boy will grow up and discover the joys — or heartaches — that come with maturation. But if we leave our heads in the sand, in denial that our sweet, innocent sons and daughters are learning about sex every day from various sources, we are failing them.

It can seem like the whole world has set itself against us in addressing the truth about sex with our kids. But we have to realize that it's only daunting when we ourselves accept as truth the lies buzzing around us. Become vigilant about identifying and denouncing the lies our culture perpetuates about sex. Choose not to believe them anymore. Proverbs 23:7 says, "As [a person] thinks within himself, so he is" (NASB). Face your fears by remembering the power of God's cleaning truth. To change the way you are, change the way you think. Romans 12:2 makes it clear: "Do not conform any longer to the pattern of this world, but be transformed by the renewing of your mind." Renew your mind by washing it with truth: God's Word.

Teach your kids by modeling what you claim to believe. Show them the joy and peace of being weird. Inspire them to want so much more than what's normal. Consistently remind them that God didn't create us to fit in — he created us to stand out. He made us to be holy, to be pure, to be set apart, to be different.

I've heard parents say, "Well, kids are going to be kids. Those are just the things they do. It's not that big of a deal. Everybody else dresses like that. Everybody else goes to those movies. Everybody else lives that way." But things are not like they were when we were kids. Things are worse. Your kids have tremendous opportunities for sin and for evil, and the temptations they face are so much greater than when you were their age. Fortunately, the opposite is also true: the next generation has more potential for righteousness for Jesus perhaps than any before it.

Young people today are deeply passionate and crave an authentic life based on truth. They're hungry to make a difference. They're willing to take a stand for whatever they believe, even to die for a cause. When they sell out to Jesus, they'll pursue a standard of righteousness that is greater than anything you and I ever saw growing up.

Don't water it down. Don't lower the standard. And don't just settle for raising it — raise it *higher*. Believe in your children. Talk with them.

Speak well of them. Encourage them. Pray for them. Celebrate the victories with them. Affirm their growth. We can raise a generation that, although they'll make mistakes, will sell out completely when Jesus grips them. They'll give him everything.

They'll make you proud by being even weirder than you are.

Part Five

VALUES

Chapter 13

GET MY DRIFT

Faith in God's revelation has nothing to do with an ideology which glorifies the status quo.

— KARL BARTH

S everal years ago our family rented a great little place right on the beach and enjoyed the vacation of a lifetime. Off the clock and on the water, we built sandcastles, got sunburned, and ate more seafood (and ice cream) than should be legal. I especially loved playing in the surf with all the kids, splashing each other, jumping waves, floating on our backs, and hearing them squeal whenever I "shark-attacked" them. In the water with them, I felt like a kid again myself as the tide washed away the accumulated stress of work, home, and church.

I knew we'd been out there on the water a long time when the sun began its colorful descent to meet the horizon. Relishing the tired-happy satisfaction that comes from hours of sand, sun, and salt water, I told the kids it was time to head back and get cleaned up for dinner. "But, Daddy," my son said, "I don't see our house anywhere!"

He was right. I scanned the beach, grasping for a point of reference, and saw only a few small homes dotting the shore. None looked like ours, though, or maybe they all looked like ours. How could our house have just disappeared like that? It was right there, we were right here, and now all of a sudden it felt like the final episode of *LOST*. At last I saw it — our little cabana probably a good quarter mile back down the beach! The entire time we were playing, the current had gently moved us downstream with the tide. We were drifting the whole time and never realized it until we couldn't find our way back.

DRIFT HAPPENS

Perhaps you've experienced a similar kind of disorientation — you thought you knew where you were in relation to something (or someone), only to look up and have no idea where they went. What happened? Obviously, none of us set out to drift away and separate ourselves from the familiar mile markers by which we navigate. But it happens all the time. It's as inevitable as the tide: if you don't focus on where you are, you will drift away from your priorities time and time again. Including your number one priority, the anchor securing all your values, beliefs, and convictions: your relationship with God.

When you glance back toward your shoreline, where are you in relationship to where you once were with God? Hebrews 2:1 says, "We must pay more careful attention ... to what we have heard, so that we do not drift away." Probably no one thinks, "You know what? I'm tired of pursuing God. Sure, he's blessed me and all, and it's really been worthwhile, but

I think it's time to just drift on downstream for a while and see where it takes me." No, more likely it simply happens the same way it happened to me and my kids at the beach. We were so caught up in having fun together that we weren't paying attention. I mean, it's not like we can actually lose something as big as a house, right? So why bother worrying about it and checking the shore every few minutes? It's not going anywhere.

Exactly. It's *not* going anywhere — we are.

The current of normalcy will pull you away from God at every opportunity if you let it. When we allow ourselves to go with the flow, literally, then we're moving away from the solid rock of God's presence in our lives. Oh, he's still there — right where he's always been and always will be. We're the ones riding the waves in pursuit of other destinations, whether we deliberately chart a course for other locales or, more likely, just allow ourselves to float away to wherever the tide takes us.

LED ASTRAY

If you're a Christian, you know that getting sidetracked from God is easy. Most do. It's perfectly normal. And you'll find lots of outside help for your heart to wander, lots of things to distract you. As you notice how people around you are living, you might find yourself questioning whether it's even worth it to follow God. It may seem like not many other people are following him. And according to Matthew 7:13 – 14, many people aren't. Perhaps worse, it seems like the people who do follow God are, well ... honestly, weird. According to that passage in Matthew 7, they're the few who are willing to do it.

Where do these kinds of thoughts come from? Have you ever considered that they might come from your spiritual enemy? Although we looked at this earlier, it's worth mentioning again: Jesus clearly identifies Satan's explicit mission — to steal, kill, and destroy (John 10:10). If you allow your enemy to steal your faith, he can destroy your life and ultimately kill your relationship with God. He's the great deceiver, the father of lies (John 8:44), so we need to be wise to his tricks (2 Cor. 2:11).

Satan specializes in destroying people's faith. And he's been using the same technique to do it — an extremely effective approach — from the very beginning. When he came to Eve in the form of a serpent, he planted the smallest seed of doubt in the ready soil of her mind. He said, "Did God *really* say ..." (Gen. 3:1, emphasis mine). Then he lied to her, essentially saying that it was God who was the liar and that God was keeping something from her (vv. 4 – 5). In other words, he weakened Eve's faith by questioning God's authority. And then he simply waited. And watched his seed grow and blossom and bear its deadly fruit.

Paul referred to this same attack when he wrote with heartfelt concern to the church at Corinth: "I am afraid that just as Eve was deceived by the serpent's cunning, your minds may somehow be led astray from your sincere and pure devotion to Christ" (2 Cor. 11:3). I feel that same concern. If you've been close to God in the past but feel distant from him now, isn't that exactly how it played out? Maybe you didn't even realize it was happening, but somehow you woke up one day and found you'd drifted. You'd been led astray from your faith in Christ.

LOSE YOUR FAITH IN 5 E-Z STEPS!

Have you ever found a piece of glass on the beach? You might not have even recognized it as glass when you first saw it. Worn by the sand, washed by the surf, and weathered by the sun and wind, glass loses its sharp edges on the beach. Over time it becomes a smooth, dull little pebble — unrecognizable from the bright, colorful shard it had been. Which is a good thing, considering we won't cut our bare feet on it. But a long way from what it, and its purpose, had been originally. Similarly, several forces will wear away at our relationship with God over time if we let them, dulling the power of our convictions and grinding us down to smooth powder.

1. Blaming God

When you're unhappy with your circumstances, it's normal to drift away from God — especially if you blame him for them. When life doesn't go the way we want, we often feel more than justified in being angry at God. Maybe I missed something in seminary, but I'm not sure where to find that passage in Scripture promising a fun, carefree life that we get to control. In fact, Jesus warned us that storms would come: "In this world you will have trouble" (John 16:33). He went on to say that the reason for his advance warning was so we'd find our peace *in him*: "Take heart! I have overcome the world." James 1:2 – 3 even tells us, "Consider it pure joy . . . whenever you face trials of many kinds, because you know that the testing of your faith develops perseverance."

It's totally weird to look forward to difficult times. But James tells us the advantage of thinking this way: "Perseverance must finish its work so that you may be mature and complete, *not lacking anything*" (James 1:4, emphasis mine). Notice one thing that these verses *don't* say: God is not the *cause* of these troubles. (More on this in a minute.)

Some of us even blame God for things that Christians do, using that as our excuse: "Well, so-and-so, who's a Christian, did *this* to me, so I'm never going to church again!" The truth is, there are almost as many different kinds of Christians as there are people. Because Christians are people. Getting angry at God for things that human beings do is a sure-fire way to drive a wedge between you and him.

Instead, consider the antidote. Proverbs 3:5 – 6 tells us, "Trust in the LORD with all your heart and lean not on your own understanding; in all your ways acknowledge him, and he will make your paths straight." Most of us are willing to trust in the Lord a little, but with all our hearts? When life is hard and feels unbearable? That's a lot to ask. And I don't know what's harder: trusting in God or not leaning on my own understanding.

2. Hanging around Bad Influences

First Corinthians 15:33 is crystal clear: "Do not be misled: 'Bad company corrupts good character.'" Yet I know so many perfectly normal people who see nothing wrong with surrounding themselves with people who couldn't care less about God. Some might even use the excuse that they're just practicing being in the world but not of the world (John 17:11 – 16). Some consider it dating evangelism, deliberately spending time with really cute unbelievers, hoping they can eventually convince them to become Christians. (I've even known people who got married with this mindset! You can probably guess how it turned out.)

After all, hanging out with strong Christians can be so annoying. They're constantly doing weird stuff: encouraging you, praying for you, trying to bless you, holding you accountable to what you say you believe. Maybe you just like to spend time with people who do bad things because they make you feel better about yourself: "At least I'm not as bad as they are." The problem with spending time with people of poor character is that they always rub off on you — and not the other way around. They pull you away from God, little by little, until you're miles away.

3. Giving In to Temptation

God doesn't cause our problems, and he doesn't tempt us. James 1:13 – 15 says, "When tempted, no one should say, 'God is tempting me.' For God cannot be tempted by evil, nor does he tempt anyone; but each one is tempted when, by his own evil desire, he is dragged away and enticed. Then, after desire has conceived, it gives birth to sin; and sin, when it is full-grown, gives birth to death." This sounds pretty serious. (And notice who's responsible: we are, because of our own desires.) It's easy to look around and see people giving in to temptation everywhere. If you live in even a modestly populated area in the United States, I'd be willing to bet that you're no more than a couple of miles from a decent cup of coffee. (In more heavily populated areas, the radius might be as little as two blocks!) We've intentionally built an entire culture around catering to the immediate gratification of our every desire. Talk about normal!

Many people think, "It's just the way I am; I can't change it. I just like having what I want as soon as possible. Everyone is this way. It's only human nature, and there's nothing wrong with it. It's totally normal!" And while they're 100 percent accurate on the latter, Paul adamantly disagrees that we have to resign ourselves to going with the flow. In Philippians 4:13, he makes it clear that you "can do everything through [Christ] who gives [you] strength."

Or maybe they just accept that it's wrong in God's eyes, although not in their own, and they'll worry about sorting it out later. If we absolutely have to bring God into our lives, then let's postpone it as long as we can and ask forgiveness later (Rom. 6:1 – 2). Others have found it easier to rename their sins with a marketing spin that would make the characters on TV's *Mad Men* proud. Instead of saying, "I struggle with pornography," they simply call it adult entertainment. Instead of being honest about cheating on their spouse, they describe their marriage as complicated. It sounds so much better — the old labels are so harsh. Romans 3:23 makes it clear that we're all guilty of sin, and Isaiah 59:2 tells us that our sin separates us from God. But this doesn't mean we have to live there.

4. Loving the World

More than just drifting from God, this force pushes off against him and fires up an outboard motor. The Bible is clear: "Do not love the world or anything in the world. If anyone loves the world, the love of the Father is not in him" (1 John 2:15). This one sounds so heavy and sobering — and it is. But the world makes it so easy to love everything here — and not only to love all the beautiful things but also to create your identity from them: "You are what you drive. You won't be happy until you build your dream house. Clothes make the man. Diamonds are a girl's best friend. If you need to go into a little debt to finance all this tasteful, fun, exciting, glamorous self-expression, then no biggie, right? I mean, you only live once, so you'd better enjoy every minute of it."

There's nothing wrong with self-expression. Unless it becomes a justification for idolatry or another version of the narcissistic god we often craft in our own image. Jesus said in Luke 12:34 that "where your treasure is, there your heart will be also." This can mean that you can put your money where you want your heart to go, like entering a destination into a GPS navigation device so it will lead you in the right direction. But this verse also means that your money functions like a GPS device in another way: if you look at where your money's going now, it will reveal your heart's present location. Do you give to people in need? Are you generous? Do you give to missions? If you pour everything you have into this life, this world, which is temporary and fading, you're jeopardizing your relationship with God, the only thing that's eternal.

5. Faking It

A common piece of business advice for start-ups is to "fake it 'til you make it." Essentially, if you give the appearance that you're successful and in demand, potential clients will perceive you this way and will want to do business with you. Normal people often apply this same "wisdom" to their faith, going through the motions of what they think the Christian life should be (or what they want it to be), even though they don't actually know God. But Jesus is very clear that faking it with God is not possible. "Not everyone who says to me, 'Lord, Lord,' will enter the kingdom of heaven, but only he who does the will of my Father who is in heaven" (Matt. 7:21). It's not like God doesn't know what's going on in your heart. What difference does it make if you fool everyone else? You can never fool God. Many people maintain their front by speaking Christianese. They have a huge, screaming fight with their spouse, yell at their kids, flip off another driver — all on the way to church! But once they pull into the parking lot, they get their game face on. They walk in smiling and shaking hands. "I'm blessed! How are you? Glory, hallelujah, brother! Isn't God so good? This is the day the Lord has made! Amen?" Another common name for this behavior is hypocrisy.

You might be thinking, "Wow, did you just bust out the h-word on me? Are you calling *me* a hypocrite?" I want to be clear. All this time, I've been talking about me. Everything I've shared here is from my own personal experience. Recently, not when I first started following Christ.

When I first became a believer, I was rabid. I was on fire. But then later, in my early days of ministry, I became an associate pastor at a great church downtown in the city where I lived. That job made perfect sense to me. I loved God so much, I figured ministry would be the perfect place for me to stay close to him. But then life started to happen, and my new job brought a lot of new pressures. It's not like I got into any kind of gross sin. I just got so busy with work that I started drifting from God without really noticing. I was faking it. I'd tell people, "I'm going to pray for you." But then I never did. People would ask me, "What's God showing you in your time with him?" And I'd make something up. I'd pull out something God had shown me years earlier. I was a hypocrite. I praised God with my lips, but my heart was far from him.

But I saw it. And I ran back to him.

LEARN THE ROPES

So how do we prevent this spiritual drift that feels so inevitable and normal? We pay attention to where we are, where we want to go, and the direction of the current. Most of all, we remain focused on our rock that never moves. And as we've seen throughout this book, it's a dedicated lifestyle that bucks the norm and dares to be weird in the best way possible — God's way. If we build anchor points throughout our lives, our heart remains tethered to our first love, God. Here are some lifelines you're probably aware of or have practiced before that I hope you'll want to resecure to your Anchor.

Read Your Bible

The easiest, most direct thing you can do is read God's story, a collection of love letters to you. Just open his Word. It's active, sharp, and alive (Heb. 4:12). His truth will pierce your heart (Acts 2:37), renew your mind (Rom. 12:2), and put you on a firm foundation (2 Tim. 2:19), one that cannot be shaken (Heb. 12:26 – 27). You should think about his Word constantly, meditating on it, mulling it over and over in your mind (Josh. 1:7 – 8).

We have more Bible resources available to us than at any time in history: multiple translations (in print, online, even on our phones!), study tools and commentaries, sermons on demand, podcasts, DVDs, and videos. If you don't know what's in the Bible, you're not even trying. In fact, if you'd like a free Bible app for your phone, you can find instructions at the end of this book on how to download YouVersion. (It really is free — no catches. My church and I are just passionate about giving away God's Word, and an app is the perfect portable format. So far we've given away over twelve million downloads! So check it out.)

Worship God

In theory, church should make connecting with God through worship easier. But apparently this is not always the case. I see normal people trying to avoid worship all the time at our church. They slip in late. They don't sing. Many stand with their hands locked at their sides (or clenched in their pockets), just spectating. It's almost like they don't realize that the Creator of the universe knows their names — and loves them. Maybe they're afraid of looking weird. David was weird. He danced for God with reckless abandon — in his underwear! (Normally I'd say, "Don't try this at home." In this case, don't try this anywhere else besides home!) And even that was just him getting started: "I'll become even more undignified than this!" (see 2 Sam. 6:14 – 23).

Some people haven't realized this, but God is outside of church buildings too. You can worship him pretty much anywhere. Even in your car. (Of course, people might think you're weird if you do.) If you made worship a part of your everyday life, how might that change your family? If you believe in God and you watch the sun rise or a bird fly or think about, you know, breathing — how could you not just break down and say, "Wow, God! You're amazing!"

Get Involved at Church

I've observed three types of people in our church. *Drop-ins* arrive at the last minute and scramble for seats, just as the music's ending (and some even later than that). They're not picky: they'll sit anywhere that's available, although they seem to prefer aisle seats and rows near the back. When whoever's speaking finishes, right at the closing prayer they slip out, usually quietly. I admire their stealth. And they're the first ones out of the parking lot.

Absorbers have achieved maximum efficiency at devouring church resources. They drink the free coffee and eat the free donuts. They're always early so they can save huge blocks of seats for family and friends in all the choice spots. They hang out in the lobby between services, "fellowshiping." Some attend multiple services, I think so their kids can get both breakfast and lunch. And they serve as little as possible.

Contributors are sometimes hard to distinguish from Absorbers. On the surface, they behave almost the same. Except Contributors seem to ration coffee and donuts. And they do serve. Like crazy. Every chance they get. They welcome people, emcee in kids' experiences, lead Bible studies in their homes, come in during the week to help the staff. I've even witnessed Contributors picking up trash that Drop-ins or Absorbers have dropped. Investors are just plain weird. Which are you?

Pray

Praying isn't hard, strange, or scary, like some people seem to think it is. At its most basic, it's just talking with God. If you had a friend you refused to talk to, eventually you couldn't keep calling that person a friend anymore. And I don't know if you know this, but talking to someone is two-way. You talk some. You listen some. Amazing things happen when you pray. Besides God listening to you and working on your behalf, your faith grows. You want more of him. So talk to him already.

NOW WHAT?

Maybe you've drifted from God. If you have, let me ask you honestly: Do you care? Or are you like that church in Sardis — dead, just pretending to be alive (Rev. 3:1)? Have you gotten used to shaking off whatever the Holy Spirit tries to say to you? Are all the things going through your head right now just going to fade? Can you read something like this and still walk away unchanged? Today is just another day. You'll go to sleep tonight, just like always. You'll wake up tomorrow, and it will be the same as today.

But maybe that's not you. Maybe you're more like the church at Ephesus that Jesus spoke to in Revelation 2:4 – 5: "You have forsaken your first love. Remember the height from which you have fallen! Repent and do the things you did at first." This is your chance. This is that moment when the Spirit of God is calling out to you. Will you listen this time? What will it take for you to get back to him?

The first part is nonnegotiable: repent. Turn away from the things you've been doing that you know have drawn you away from God. Prepare your heart. Get your soil healthy, ready to receive from him again. Then what happens next depends: what were the things you were doing before when you were close to him? Go back and do those things again. Start there and see where he leads you. Maybe you'll stop eating and start a fast. Maybe you're going to stay up all night long, with your Bible open and your face on the carpet. Your eyes are going to get puffy. If you wear makeup, it's going to get smudged. You're going to cry. You're going to hurt for a while.

I can promise you this: If you really, sincerely, genuinely want God back, he hasn't moved. He's still there, just like always, ready to bear-hug you again, just like in the old days. His word straight to you is from Jeremiah 29:12 – 13: "You will call upon me and come and pray to me, and I will listen to you. You will seek me and find me when you seek me with all your heart."

Then, once his Word has landed in your heart, it will overflow thirty, sixty, or a hundred times. Instead of drifting away from God, you'll be firmly anchored, able to swim against the tide, offering living water to all you meet.

Chapter 14

A WEIRD BLESSING

No one is useless in the world who lightens the burden of it for anyone else.

— CHARLES DICKENS

Early in my ministry as an associate pastor, I would often fill in for other preachers. One week, my friend Paul invited me to speak to his church while he was on vacation.

Sporting my best (and only) suit, with my shirt ironed and shoes polished to complete the first impression, I arrived plenty early and was immediately greeted at the side door by Lora, the church secretary.

"I've got great news!" she said, beaming. "We're having a visitor at church today — so you better preach great!"

Now, I'm all for getting excited when visitors come to church, but it was evident from Lora's over-the-top enthusiasm that they were rare commodities at this small, aging church on the south side of our town. As the community had suffered decline, the church kept pace with it, and Paul had confided more than once that he feared the doors might not stay open forever.

Curious, I asked Lora how she knew that a guest would be joining us. She said that a woman had called the church that morning and asked for directions. The caller explained that she'd fallen on hard times and wanted to give church a try. Lora prayed with the caller and said she'd be sure to look for her in the service. Armed with a little extra motivation, I too prayed and asked God to use me to minister to this hurting lady who would be visiting the church for the first time.

Just before the service started, Lora stationed me by the church's big wooden front doors alongside another pillar from the congregation, an older man named Virgil.

Within moments, I could tell Virgil loved his church and took his post at the big wooden doors seriously. In between greeting the few dozen members trickling into the building, he started a running monologue about the problems with today's generation. "They're rebellious!" Virgil barked, complaining that young people aren't respectful of God and his church.

In the middle of Virgil's rant, I saw her — the visitor — drive up in a beat-up older car so dirty that I couldn't tell if it was light gray or faded blue. Its balding tires, low in air pressure, squeaked as she turned into a parking spot. Getting out, she revealed a very dented driver-side door. Saying that she stood out is an understatement.

While everyone else entering the church that morning wore suits (dated as they were) or dresses (most ankle length), our visitor closed her car door with a cigarette in her hand and displayed an ensemble of tight blue jeans and a slightly tighter sleeveless shirt, which — forgive me for noticing — definitely revealed much more than the apparel of the average female Sunday school teacher. She might have been attractive if life had been kinder to her. Without judging her, I found my mind pinballing with possibilities: Abusive boyfriend? Drug addiction? Unemployment? Depression? Abandonment? All of these and more?

As she walked toward the church, she took a deep breath and tilted her head slightly, looking up at Virgil and me. I prayed again, asking God to give me the words to say that might encourage her with his hope.

My silent prayer was interrupted as Virgil hurled his welcome grenade at the young woman. "We wear our best clothes for God at this church. Is that the best outfit you own? Or do you just not care what God thinks?"

"Nooooo!" I desperately wanted to shout. Time collapsed into slow motion, as if I were suddenly caught up in an action-suspense movie and Virgil had just pressed the detonation button for the bomb beneath us all.

My mind scrambled for the best way to undo Virgil's assault. I considered smiling and yelling out, "Don't mind old Virgil here — he's a little …" and making the cuckoo gesture. Then I thought about laughing really loud and saying, "I think we got her — she really thinks you're serious! Come on in, miss. Uncle Virgil's just been watching too much *Punk'd!*" The darkest part of me, though, wanted to assume the Jason Bourne role and launch myself at Virgil with a punch so hard that he'd meet God face-to-face. (I realize this would not exactly honor Christ and offer the visitor any better reason to stick around.) Instead, I just stood there, frozen in place by my own outrage and uncertainty.

As if on cue, the visitor simply turned, walked back to her clunker of a car, and drove away.

Virgil mumbled, "Rebellious."

A BURDEN IN DISGUISE

Something happened in my heart that moment. Before God, I made several promises that I vowed to keep for the rest of my life. I committed to resist judging someone who doesn't know God. I promised never to turn anyone away from church because of the way they look. I vowed never to become someone like Virgil.

Silently I turned my back to him and walked back into the secretary's office, overcome with emotion. As strange as it sounds, I seemed to feel God's pain. The hurt I experienced seemed bigger than my own. Lora asked me what happened, and fighting back my tears, I told her how Virgil turned away the hurting visitor. She teared up too and asked if she could pray for me.

I don't remember all that she said, but I'll never forget one thing. She asked God to use this experience to help my heart break forever for those who don't know Christ. The whole morning had not been anything like I expected, and I was a bit stunned by her prayer. Nonetheless, I felt like she had just given me a strange gift — something well-intentioned that was infinitely more valuable than whatever I might have asked for.

I realized that day that blessings come in a variety of shapes, colors, and sizes. It's normal to give thanks for the good things: "Thank you, God, for blessing me with great health." "I'm so grateful — I got a raise!" "God has blessed us with another child. This time it's a girl." "God gave us a great deal on a new home. What a blessing!"

God's blessings, however, aren't always bigger, better, and beautiful. In fact, I truly believe that God gifts his chosen leaders with a very unusual blessing. You might even call it a weird blessing because most of the time we call it ... a burden.

WHAT'S YOUR BURDEN?

Remember Popeye the Sailor Man? You know, "who fights to the finish, 'cause he eats his spinach — he's Popeye the Sailor Man! Toot! Toot!" (I'm really sorry if this song gets stuck in your head the rest of the day.) Whenever his archenemy, Brutus, attacked, kidnapped, or insulted Popeye's faithful girlfriend, Olive Oyl, our hero would finally reach his limit and shout, "That's all I can stands; I can't stands no more!" So he'd swallow a can of spinach and crush Brutus.

I'm asking God to give you a Popeye moment. A moment when God blesses you with a divine burden: something that bothers you so deeply, you're moved from complacency to action. Bill Hybels calls this "divine discontent" in his powerful book by the same title. I'm asking God to bless you with something that unsettles you, disturbs you, and upsets you.

If you listen, God will show you something that makes your heart ache on behalf of his. He will bless you with a burden.

If you're like most normal people, you're probably wondering, "Why in the world would I want a burden?" Most of us feel good when we avoid burdens — after all, isn't life hard enough? Why ask God for more trials, trauma, and tears? It's normal to want to avoid pain — human even. But God didn't put us here on earth just to feel good and enjoy ourselves. He doesn't give us our lives so we can master techniques in avoiding pain.

> **If you listen, God will show you something that makes your heart ache on behalf of his. He will bless you with a burden.**

He puts us here to make an eternal difference.

He puts us here to show everyone around us how much he loves them.

He puts us here to be his hands and feet, his body and his heart.

Most of us enjoy the traditional blessings that come our way. If you travel to a nice resort for vacation or have a day on the lake skiing, you're grateful for the gift. If you drive a reliable car, enjoy a cool pair of sunglasses, or purchase your favorite song on iTunes, you probably get a nice feeling for a while. If you meet an admired celebrity, get a promotion, or win a door prize at your office party, you're probably thrilled.

Special as they are, though, these blessings don't seem to fulfill us very long. We take pleasure in the moment or the days or weeks following, but the pleasure often fades. Or worse, we begin to feel entitled and act like a spoiled child, not only expecting blessings but also demanding them as divine perks.

On the other hand, when you do something for someone else, there's often a greater, deeper satisfaction. When God uses you to right a wrong, you experience something that's longer lasting and more meaningful. When you give of yourself in a way that reflects God's goodness, blesses someone else, and makes the world better, you're taken out of yourself and reminded that your purpose is not about feeling good all the time. You feel alive and whole, humbled and privileged, rich in peace and close to God.

If we want to grow closer to God, if we want our values to be his values, then we need to become vigilant for opportunities where he wants to bless us with a burden. He wants to move us beyond our self-focused, normal understanding of his blessings and into an others-focused, extraordinary experience of his character. We reflect God's character the most when we give freely of ourselves with no strings attached, no secret motives, no hidden agenda. No return benefit other than pleasing our Father by sharing his love with his other children. If you aren't already blessed with a weird burden, I pray God will bless you with one soon. Whether or not you have one yet, I want to share three areas that can provide some muscle-building spinach for all your Popeye moments.

1. Building Blocks and Broken Pieces

What breaks your heart? What is it in life that moves you to tears or turns your stomach? What injustice crushes you and, if you let it, will keep you awake at night?

Nehemiah is one of the best examples in the Bible of a heartbroken man blessed with a divine burden. When he found out that the walls of his (and God's) beloved city, Jerusalem, were destroyed, he became distraught. Suddenly God's people were vulnerable to attack, and Nehemiah could barely stomach his discomfort: "They said to me, '… The wall of Jerusalem is broken down, and its gates have been burned with fire.' When I heard these things, I sat down and wept. For some days I mourned and fasted and prayed before the God of heaven" (Neh. 1:3 – 4). He was so shaken that he was moved to tears. Not only did he unleash his emotion through rivers of tears, but for several days he denied his body food so he could pray and seek the God of heaven. Through Nehemiah's sense of loss, and his fear of the potential consequences, he discovered God was blessing him with an unusual blessing — a burden to rebuild the walls.

When I think of weird blessings and broken hearts, I also think of Dr. Martin Luther King Jr. This great man became so distraught over racial injustice and other wounds of prejudice that he was willing to do anything and everything possible to right this wrong. His famous, soul-stirring "I have a dream" speech will still give you chills and break your heart today. Decades later, long after his life on earth tragically ended, the legacy of his burden lives on, improving lives for generations to come. All because one man allowed his burden to birth a dream.

We see so many people in need today that we can easily become callous with acceptance and indifference. When was the last time you felt your heart pierced by the plight of another person? At the busy intersection when the homeless woman looked you in the eye? When you met the fifth-grader embarrassed because he'd never learned to read in his inner-city school? When the young teen girl giving you a manicure shared about her unexpected pregnancy?

What is it that strikes a blow to your heart when you hear about it? Do you see impoverished people and tear up over all they lack? Does homelessness make you ache? Do you know an unwed mom whose struggles feel like your own? Did you read an article about children with AIDS and feel compelled to do something immediately? Pause for a moment and prayerfully consider your response: What breaks your heart?

2. A Righteous Anger

Here's another question that will help identify and empower our passion for a divinely given burden: What makes you angry?

We're not talking about your pet peeves (like when someone leaves the toilet seat up or answers a cell phone during the movie). Nor are we talking about supersized abstractions like war, terrorism, or global warming. These larger issues may be a good starting point, but I'm hoping you'll uncover something specific that makes you righteously angry, something that moves you on behalf of God.

While Nehemiah encapsulates the brokenhearted, Moses offers us the perfect picture of a person channeling his righteous anger in an effective direction. Since he was a Hebrew raised in an Egyptian home, Moses always had a heart for his people. One day when he happened upon an Egyptian beating a Hebrew slave, something inside him snapped. He had a Popeye moment of epic proportions and couldn't "stands it no more." Unable to contain his emotion, Moses unleashed his outrage on the Egyptian, taking his life (Exod. 2:12). While this was not the right way to respond to the situation, Moses clearly demonstrated the passionate power needed to lead his people's exodus from the land. So it's not surprising, then, years later, that God chose Moses to confront Pharaoh and demand his people's freedom. Just as God used Nehemiah to do what others considered impossible, so God used Moses to lead the Israelites out of Egyptian slavery — simply because God ignited a burden in his heart.

Can you relate to the intensity of Moses' response to the Egyptian slave owner? What is it that makes you so angry, bothers you so deeply, that you're compelled to act? Are you angry when you see the elderly dishonored, disrespected, and uncared for? Do you hate pornography and other sexual addictions, knowing how they destroy lives by the thousands? Do you despise corrupt politicians, who lack integrity and values? Do you hate it when new Christians are left to fend for themselves and no one helps them to mature?

Some Christians think they should never be angry. But the Bible actually tells us that when we are angry, we should simply avoid sin (Eph. 4:26). If something makes you divinely angry, don't avoid it. Mother Teresa once said, "When I see waste, I feel angry on the inside. I don't approve of myself getting angry, but it's something you can't help after seeing Ethiopia!"

3. When You Care Enough to Send the Very Best

Many people may be heartbroken, but not enough to take action. Others may be outraged and rant about the problem frequently but offer no solutions. If you really want to discover and develop the burden that uniquely connects you to the heart of God, you have to have courage. You have to risk. You have to do something — anything — to alleviate the suffering you've identified and embraced as your own.

In the Old Testament, a young shepherd is a great example of someone who cared while others wouldn't act. The Philistine army picked its fiercest warrior, a nine- or ten-foot monster of a man named Goliath. This giant, according to battle traditions, challenged anyone from Israel to a duel. Whoever lived, won. And the winner's side became the victor in the war.

Not surprisingly, all the normal-sized men didn't want to fight the UFC champion of all time. I'm not saying they didn't care. I'm sure they did. They just didn't care enough to send their very best — their own lives on the line.

Along came a teenage shepherd boy, however, who would make Hallmark proud. Young David, who should've been tending sheep, was dumbfounded that no one would stand up and fight. Since he was a servant of God Most High, David believed that God would do battle with him and for him. The young shepherd warrior boldly asked, "Who is this uncircumcised Philistine that he should defy the armies of the living God?" (1 Sam. 17:26). While everyone else thought Goliath was too big to beat, David picked up five smooth stones and thought, *With God's help, he's too big to miss.* And sure enough, David cared enough to sling a rock. You know the end of the story.

I bet if you stop for a moment, you'll quickly recognize something you care about that others aren't willing to face or don't even seem to recognize. Maybe you constantly want to help the people who help those addicted to drugs or alcohol. Maybe you care deeply for veterans who are handicapped from serving in Iraq or Afghanistan. Perhaps you stay awake at night thinking about how you can help other people afford to adopt. Or how you can treat a hundred underprivileged inner-city kids to a new baseball glove and a day at the nearest major-league park for a home game.

When you feel this burden, you might be frustrated, wondering why no one else cares as much as you do. The reason why you care and others don't could be because God has aimed it directly at you. Maybe it's because of what you've been exposed to, maybe it's because of a way you've been hurt, or maybe it's something you simply can't explain. Whatever the reason, you care, and you care deeply. You care because God gave you this unusual blessing: a burden to make a difference.

NAME IT TO CLAIM IT

About ten years ago, as part of a series on the importance of having a God-given vision, I asked about a hundred leaders from our church an important question:

"If money were no object to you, what would you do with the rest of your life?"

Knowing how responses to this question can truly reveal a person's greatest passion, I fully expected beautiful, life-changing answers: "I'd volunteer at the crisis pregnancy center." "I'd serve in an orphanage in Haiti." "I'd mentor inner-city kids."

Boy, was I in for a shock. Instead of giving these kinds of others-centered answers, the vast majority responded like retiring CEOs: "I'd travel." "I'd get a bigger house." "I'd buy a boat."

It really surprised me. *Why are their biggest dreams and goals self-centered?* I wanted to lock them all in a room and ask, "Do you really think that God sent Jesus to bleed and die for our sins so our biggest dream in life would be to get a new boat?" As disappointed as I was in their responses, in some ways I was responsible. God had given me the privilege to spiritually nurture and shepherd the flock. Evidently, I had plenty of room to improve.

As I reflected on their dreams, it suddenly made more sense.

Normal people want to live a burden-free life. By nature, we tend to think of ourselves first. It's unquestionably normal. But thankfully, God didn't call us to be normal. Paul said in Ephesians that "we are God's workmanship [or masterpiece], created in Christ Jesus to do good works, which God prepared in advance for us to do" (Eph. 2:10). Imagine: before you were born, God knew what he wanted you to do. God decided that this time in history was perfect for you to glorify him and make an eternal difference. So God gave you unique gifts, talents, passions, and experiences to propel you into your life purpose.

Instead of living for normal blessings, what if you took a moment to give your newest (and admittedly odd) blessing a name. God put you on earth with a divine assignment — something prepared in advance for you to do. I've found that the things that make us sad, the things that make us righteously angry, or the things we care about that others don't are often a key that unlocks our reason for living. It's our burden.

So how about it? What's yours? Think about it. And give life to it. What is your burden? Say it out loud or, if you'd like, write it in the blank.

"My weird blessing is to have a burden for _____."

EVERY STARFISH MATTERS

One day an older gentleman was strolling down the beach and saw a young boy frantically picking up stranded starfish and throwing them back into the ocean. Noticing hundreds, if not thousands, of displaced starfish washed up on shore, the polite gentleman laughed softly as he approached the eager boy. "Hey there, youngster," he said compassionately. "You really shouldn't waste your time. There's too many of them. You'll never be able to make a difference."

Looking up, the boy held a single starfish in his palm and suddenly hurled the creature full force back into the ocean. "I made a difference to that one!" he said and continued on his mission.

When you break out of the normal mode and allow your burden to grow, chances are good that it will feel futile at times. You'll hear a voice chiding, "You might as well give up. You can't change anything. What difference is this really going to make?"

When you hear this voice of doubt, remember, you can't do every-thing, but you can do something. Every starfish matters.

As your burden grows, as it begins to break your heart and open your eyes, don't hesitate to take action. Like Nehemiah, you might weep, fast, and pray. Then get up and do something. Ask for help. Raise some money. Take a trip. Write a chapter. Start a blog. Foster a child. Become a Big Brother. Launch a ministry. Do something. You can't do everything. But you can do something.

Years ago someone wrote this powerful prayer. It's my prayer for all of us who long for more than just the gratification of normal blessings.

> *May God bless you with discomfort at easy answers, half truths, and superficial relationships, so that you may live deep within your heart. May God bless you with anger at injustice, oppression, and exploitation of people, so that you may work for justice, freedom, and peace. May God bless you with tears to shed for those who suffer from pain, rejection, and starvation, so that you may reach out your hand to comfort them and to turn their pain into joy. And may God bless you with enough foolishness to believe that you can make a difference in this world, so that you can do what others claim cannot be done. May God bless you with the weirdest blessing possible — his divine burden.*

Chapter 15

JUST ONE THING

Often he who does too much does too little.

— ITALIAN PROVERB

O n New Year's Eve, I often have that feeling: "Wow, that year went by *so* fast!" Most of the time, I look forward to the coming year with excitement and anticipation for all God has in store. But other years, I can't help thinking, "Man, I'm *so* glad that year is over!" Both are pretty normal, I suspect.

It's also quite normal to make New Year's resolutions — often things like losing weight or giving up smoking, spending more time with family or starting a new project. Unfortunately, by the end of January, 40 percent of people who made New Year's resolutions break them. By Valentine's Day, the number of those who cannot sustain what they started jumps to 75 percent. I've made and broken my share of resolutions, but in the last few years I've changed my New Year's ritual in a positively weird way. Instead of making a long list of resolutions for myself, I make only one resolution that's chosen by someone else.

At the beginning of a new year, as well as during other life seasons, many of us try to imagine all the things we'd like to be different about our lives, and we try to tackle them all at once. Some people might even try to get organized and make lists capturing their goals and action points. Usually, though, we spend more time making those lists than we do actually following up and doing the items on them. Most people have a lot of unfinished ideas — myself included.

So I knew that if I was truly going to change, and change in the right direction of being more like Jesus, then I needed a different approach. A weird approach. So several years ago I began a personal discipline to limit my life's focus, to concentrate all my attention on fulfilling just a handful of goals. In the months leading up to a new year, I'll pray constantly, asking God, "What is the *one thing* you want to be different in my life next year?" Rather than ending up with a long list of New Year's resolutions, I focus on the one thing he reveals to me. Since I trust God's wisdom to direct my path more than I trust my own good intentions, I'm purposeful and intentional about asking (and listening to) him for just one thing.

One thing may not sound like a big deal to you. But think about it. If you set out to change several things all in one year — and you don't fully accomplish any of them — what was the point? Why bother if you're only setting yourself up to fail yet again? So consider the weird alternative: if you can change just one thing in your life — and you change that one thing entirely, fully, completely — then over the course of a decade, the landscape of your life will look dramatically different. Ten cumulative one things. Ten major changes. Ten disciplines. Ten steps closer to who God wants you to be. A decade of one things adds up to a changed life.

PAVED WITH GOD INTENTIONS

Most of us have good intentions about following through on our resolutions. But as you and I both know, good intentions can't change us or improve our lives without action. It's normal to make resolutions, have good intentions to keep them, maybe even keep them for a while, but ultimately let them slip away. If we want to be better than normal, we must move from good intentions to what I call God intentions.

Good intentions are the ideas we have that motivate us to set and achieve the goals that we seriously, genuinely want to accomplish. God intentions go way beyond this, because they rely on discovering and acting on what *he* wants us to do. Whereas good intentions are what we come up with, God intentions are our Father's ideas.

If we want to be better than normal, we must move from good intentions to what I call God intentions.

How can you find out God's intentions? You can ask him what he wants for you. If you'll listen to the Spirit of God, I believe, he'll speak directly to you and show you that *one* thing that he wants for you and from you, what he wants to do in your life. Instead of having just good intentions that are me-centered, you can have God intentions that are God-centered. And when God puts something into you, you can be certain it will come to pass.

Alongside finding my "one thing" focus each New Year's, I always review the forty-third chapter of Isaiah, in which God gives the people of Israel a series of beautiful, powerful promises. In verses 18 and 19, he makes one particularly life-changing promise, one that I believe applies equally to you and me today: "Forget the former things; do not dwell on the past. See, I am doing a new thing! Now it springs up; do you not perceive it? I am making a way in the desert and streams in the wasteland."

Maybe God wants to do a new thing for you. Something different. Something weird. Maybe he isn't waiting until New Year's to reveal it to you — maybe he's starting right now.

U + 4 = 1

If you're serious about wanting to know where God wants you to focus your attention right now, then four questions can help provide clarity during your discernment. As you focus in on discovering your one thing, ask yourself the following. You may find that it helps to write down your responses to each, discuss them with someone you trust who knows you well, and pray through each of them, listening intently for God's voice.

1. What One Thing Do You Desire from God?

If God were to offer you, "I'll do any one thing that you ask," what would you ask for?

During the course of his lifetime, and as recorded throughout Scripture, David asked God for many different things — strength, courage, victory over enemies, help for his children, forgiveness. Among them all, however, there's one prayer in which David narrowed his focus and distilled his desires into a singular request: "*One thing* I ask of the LORD, this is what I seek: that I may dwell in the house of the LORD all the days of my life, to gaze upon the beauty of the LORD and to seek him in his temple" (Ps. 27:4, emphasis mine). The Bible describes David as a man after God's own heart, and this verse goes a long way in revealing why. David cuts through all the many needs, wants, and desires that may have been bouncing around inside him and essentially says, "If I could have only *one thing*, I want to be with God, to be in his presence, to know that he is always with me." Whether in good times or bad times, David knew the thing he needed most: to feel God's presence close by, intimately, through worship.

What one thing do you desire from God?

A few years ago I faced some good problems to have. Our church was growing, and almost every day we saw people's lives being changed. The need to know how to handle the growth and find the right leaders weighed heavily on me. Recalling that God offered to grant King Solomon whatever he asked for (2 Chron. 1:7 – 10), I asked God for the same thing Solomon did — wisdom. I began praying, "Father, this is too much. I'm struggling. This year, right now, please give me wisdom."

God directed me to the book of Proverbs. I started reading one chapter every day, which I did for a year. Since Proverbs has 31 chapters, this means I read through the entire book twelve times that year. God promises us that if we lack wisdom and ask him for it, he will give it to us (James 1:5). And he began giving it to me. This also helps explain why I've included so many verses from Proverbs in this book!

What's your one desire? Maybe someone close to you is not a believer, and the one thing you want is for God to use you in bringing this person into a relationship with Christ. Maybe you're struggling with an addiction or some other stronghold, and it's keeping you from deepening your own relationship with God.

Or perhaps when you look at your marriage, you know it's not where God wants it to be. You might be tempted to ask God to fix the other person in your relationship. Instead, consider praying, "Lord, please change my heart. Please make me the person you want me to be. As much as it depends on me, please give me the grace to live peacefully with my spouse. And please heal our marriage."

Maybe it's time to slow down finally and honor the promise you've been making — and breaking — to your family for years. Time fast-forwards as your kids grow up, your spouse ages, your friends come and go. And you're missing it — lost in the commute, the office, the business trips, the household chores, the bills, the obligations, and all the rest that life seems to demand so urgently. Is this really how you want to live your life? Is this really how God wants you to live?

Maybe you're not married, and it feels like everyone around you is. You're happy for them, but at the same time it's making you feel so alone. You may even really desire somebody for yourself, but it's just not working out right now. Maybe you should try praying, "Father, please be enough for me. Please help me to be completely satisfied with you."

What one thing do you desire from God?

2. What One Thing Do You Lack?

If you can be honest about your spiritual life, your relationship with God, what one thing is missing? Remember the story about the young rich guy who sought out Jesus for some advice?

He asks, "Jesus, what do I need to do to inherit eternal life?"

Jesus answers, "You need to obey the commandments."

Our wealthy up-and-comer replies, "Check, check, check, check — I've done all of those things."

Jesus, of course, can see through the young man's outward obedience, directly into his heart. And there he sees a problem the young man isn't even aware of. Then Jesus tells him something he never said to anybody else. Mark 10:21 tells us, "Jesus looked at him and loved him. 'One thing you lack,' he said. 'Go, sell everything you have and give to the poor, and you will have treasure in heaven. Then come, follow me.'"

This story fascinates me for several reasons. First, it's clearly stated that Jesus loved this guy. His answer was going to be difficult for the young man to hear, so Jesus made sure to frame it in love. Second, Christ offered this guy the opportunity to follow him. Besides the disciples, Jesus never offered this to anyone else. Finally, Jesus boiled the whole problem down to the one thing that the young man lacked. Not two things. Not dozens of things. Just one.

For many of us, it's just one thing standing in our way of completely following Jesus. For this guy, it was material possessions, his belief that wealth could bring him security. But he just couldn't let go, even when God specifically showed him the one thing he lacked. He was unwilling to do the one thing that would have spiritually benefited him most, and he went away sad.

If we're honest with ourselves, most of us know the one thing we lack. Has there been an issue that God keeps putting on your heart again and again? Maybe you've fought it or just ignored it, but you've never addressed it. It's time. What is Jesus saying to you about the one thing you lack?

It could be simply spending time in God's Word. You used to do it, and then your life hit Mach 1 with a spouse and new job, and then kids and moving — there's just not time. Or maybe you grew up reading the Bible so frequently that it just doesn't seem as important or as fresh as it once did.

Maybe you've been going to church for a long time, but you've never bothered to make Christian friends, to find fellowship, to surround yourself with other people who can pray for you and hold you accountable. Maybe you keep meaning to, but you just haven't started yet. Maybe you're resisting because you're shy or you feel inadequate or you just don't know where to start. But deep down, you *know*: that one thing could be the catalyst that helps you finally take off spiritually.

Some people really wrestle with the whole idea of tithing. You may have heard people say, "Give God your first and best, and trust him to bless the rest." You've read the Bible verses about giving. You know what it says. You know it's the right thing to do. You just have to answer for yourself once and for all: "Do I really believe those words — or not?" God's asking, "Are you going to trust me?"

Maybe you know that you need someone to hold you accountable.

Without someone speaking into your life and keeping you on track with the things you believe, you have a tendency to drift into habitual sin — and you recognize this about yourself.

What's hindering your relationship with God? What one thing do you lack?

3. What One Thing Do You Need to Let Go?

As we've seen, normal people hold on to just about everything — busyness, money, possessions, grudges. Maybe it's time to get weird and do something different — and let one big thing go. In Philippians 3:7 – 11, the apostle Paul shares passionately about how much he desires not simply to know about Christ but also to *know* him, to the point where he even wants to share in his suffering. Then he explains what's necessary for this to take place: "Brothers, I do not consider myself yet to have taken hold of it. But *one thing* I do: Forgetting what is behind and straining toward what is ahead, I press on toward the goal to win the prize for which God has called me heavenward in Christ Jesus" (vv. 13 – 14, emphasis mine).

Paul's one thing was committing to forget about the past, to forge ahead into the future. In a single decision, in one fluid action, he releases the past and moves forward, no matter the consequences.

How was Paul's past hindering his knowing Christ? Unfortunately, we don't know specifically; the Scriptures don't tell us. But we do know some things that happened in his past. He witnessed a crowd stoning Stephen, the first Christian martyr. Maybe he wanted to put that behind him. When he was known as Saul, Paul had relished the authority he'd received from the synagogue elders to chase down Christians, persecuting them, imprisoning them, and even executing them. Maybe he wanted to forget those wrongs. Or maybe it was the physical and psychological pain he himself had endured as he was persecuted for his own faith in Christ: the jail time, the beatings, the shipwrecks. Maybe for each of these times that Paul had faced hardship, that he had been unjustly accused and punished, he wanted to forget, to forgive his accusers, to just let those things go and move ahead. Moving forward in this way takes discipline and focus.

If you're not moving forward, not headed where God wants you to be, maybe it's because you're holding on to something from the past. It's time to let go. Someone hurt you. You're holding anger and bitterness, a refusal to forgive. An understandable, normal response. But God wants to do something new. You can't dwell in the past; you have to forget what's behind, and you have to press on. I'm convinced that one of the biggest challenges in marriages today is that people simply won't let go of the past. Someone hurt you in the past, so you continue to punish them for what they did.

Maybe it wasn't someone else who let you down. Maybe you feel like you let yourself down. Maybe you failed at something, and now you believe you're a failure because you messed up. It could have been engaging in sexual immorality or betraying your business partner, cheating the government or slandering a friend you secretly resent. But it's time you confess it, ask for forgiveness (from God and anyone affected), and let it go. Then it's over. You move forward. You release the pain of the past and press on. It's a new day, and God is doing a new thing. He wants to take you to a new place, to transform you into a new person. What one thing do you need to let go?

4. What One Promise Do You Need to Claim?

Maybe you feel that God has already shown you a vision for your future — you know that he's leading you somewhere, that he's up to something. But it still hasn't happened yet. You find yourself constantly asking, "Where are you, God?" David knew this feeling quite well. In the Old Testament (1 Samuel 16), David was a young man when Samuel anointed him as

Israel's next king. Basically, Samuel traveled to Bethlehem and looked over each of Jesse's sons, as God had told him to. When Samuel saw Eliab, God told him, "Do not consider his appearance or his height, for I have rejected him. The LORD does not look at the things man looks at. Man looks at the outward appearance, but the LORD looks at the heart" (v. 7).

So Samuel was like, "Handsome, sure. But that's not him. Next. He's talented ... but no. This one's strong — no, sorry. Who *else* do you have?"

Jesse more or less answered, "Well, the runt is out there taking care of sheep."

So Samuel sent for him. When Samuel laid eyes on David, God said, "Rise and anoint him; he is the one" (v. 12). God had made the promise that David would be the next king over Israel.

Just as soon as he was anointed, however, it seemed like he'd take one step forward ... and two steps back. David would see a victory, and Saul would come in right behind him, trying to run him down and destroy him. David had to be thinking, "I just don't see it, God. I know this is what you said was going to happen, but what's the holdup?"

We mustn't lose the hope of a specific promise that God has given us. It may not look like we expect it to look (who expected the Messiah to be born in a manger?), or arrive when we want it to arrive (who knew Abraham and Sarah could have kids in their old age?), but God is always faithful to his word. Romans 8:31 – 32 says, "If God is for us, who can be against us? He who did not spare his own Son, but gave him up for us all — how will he not also, along with him, graciously give us all things?" Because this one promise is true, even if you don't see anything else in your life working the way you think it should, it's enough! God is still in control. And he is for you. You just have to be patient.

Easier said than done, I know. When our church was still really young, I remember a time when I began to have all kinds of physical problems. Behind the scenes, I was anxious and terrified because I knew that the church had outgrown my leadership abilities. Finally I realized the main problem: I was relying too much on my own abilities. I got on my face before God and started talking to him: "Father, please help us. I'm so weak. I don't know what to do. Everything I have to offer to this ministry is completely inadequate. I'm not smart enough to do this. I'm not good enough. Please help!" That year, God gave me one promise that to this day I still hold close: "My grace is sufficient for you, for my power is made perfect in weakness" (2 Cor. 12:9). Ever since then, for more than ten years now, we haven't been building our church on our strengths; we've been building it on our weaknesses. It's only in the weaknesses that God's strength, his power, is made perfect. I can't tell you how many times I've reminded God of that promise and asked him to fulfill it in our lives.

What one promise from God do you need to claim?

ONE FOR ALL

I'm willing to admit: there are plenty of things I don't know. But this doesn't matter. What matters is the one thing I do know for certain: God is with me. He's with you too, even right now as you read these words. He's for you and wants to help you be the person he created you to be. He is the one for all of us.

We don't have to carry heavy loads that constantly weigh us down and hold us back. We don't have to take on a dozen new goals to prove to others, or to God, that we're strong enough to change. We don't have to fix ourselves. We have only to remain focused on our pearl of great price, the single gem embodying what we truly long for. Reflect on all the thoughts and feelings that this chapter, I hope, has stirred in you.

What one thing do you desire from God above all else? Focus. Be specific. Be honest.

What one thing is the Holy Spirit showing you that you lack? Will you have the courage to obey the voice of God?

What one thing do you need to let go? It's time. Forget it. Press forward.

What one promise do you need to claim? Find it. Don't give up. Cling to it.

Normal people attempt countless goals with limited success. Weird people focus on just one God-given objective with tremendous results. Instead of trying to take in the entire scope of your life's mural, maybe it's time to zero in on one major detail, one significant color, one delicate brushstroke. Focus all your attention on it. Let God create in you his masterpiece. He will make you truly different and joyfully weird.

WEIRDER THAN NORMAL

Lukewarm acceptance is more bewildering than outright rejection.

— MARTIN LUTHER KING JR.

I recently took my daughter Anna to get her ears pierced at the mall for her birthday. After picking out her first pair of earrings, she sat quietly in the chair as a woman who was clearly a professional piercer aimed her device (which looked to me like a small staple gun) at my sweet birthday girl's lobes. Anna smiled up at me, bravely enduring the pain without a trace of fear.

With her ears now proudly bedazzled, Anna led me to our next destination on the birthday circuit — the candy store. We got her favorite kind, of course, as well as another flavor I thought she might share with her brothers and sisters (okay, at least her sisters), and a couple of other kinds for me (just to show her I was in the birthday spirit). Waiting our turn in line to pay, I marveled at the selection of every gummy creature imaginable — who knew there was such a market for candy rodents? The chocolate-covered dog bone held special interest, and I contemplated buying it to psych out Amy and the kids.

"Hey, Anna — look at this dog treat! How funny is that?" I said. When I turned to my daughter, her face was a pale shade of green — and growing greener.

"Daddy, I'm about to throw up," she whispered. Evidently, the trauma of her ear piercing had caught up to her. Without wasting a second, I scooped her up Jack Bauer – style and sprinted to a garbage can I'd spied earlier. Like a small volcano erupting, she vomited *everywhere*. The violent kind of uncontrollable projectile vomiting. *Everywhere.*

PART-TIME LOVER

Years ago, as I wrestled through caring too much about what people think, God showed me something that left me feeling as sick as Anna after her ear piercing. As I fretted and stewed about whether this person liked my sermon that week or why so many members seemed to have the gift of criticism, I realized that I had become a full-time pastor and a part-time Christian.

I was devastated and knew I had to refocus on my first love if I was ever going to be more like Christ and minister effectively to others in his name. Maybe you can relate. Your multiple roles could each be a full-time job, collectively elbowing out time and attention for your faith. Maybe you're a full-time mom and a part-time follower of Christ. The children take so much out of you. Every day is a constant struggle just to keep up: schoolwork, baths, laundry, cooking, shopping, housecleaning, car pooling.

Maybe you're a full-time businessperson and a part-time follower of Christ. You're really good at what you do, a savvy entrepreneur with a talent for making money. You feel blessed that you get to do what you love to make a living. Could be that you're a full-time musician and a part-time follower of Christ. You've even said many times, "Music is my life." You play, practice, write, hear the world around you in notes, chords, lyrics. Or maybe you're a full-time student, part-time follower of Christ. You have classes and grades to keep up with, and probably a job too.

Regardless of the situation, you're painfully aware that your faith isn't the priority it once was, if it's a priority at all. You never meant for it to happen, but you just woke up one day and suddenly realized that your passion for God was gone. You still believe in God. You even believe in Jesus and what he's done for you. There are just too many other pulls and shoves on your life. Full-time lover of your world; part-time lover of God.

You've become lukewarm. God says this makes him want to puke.

ROOM TEMPERATURE

My concern with our culture and primary motivation for writing this book is that we've made lukewarm synonymous with normal. "The Lord says: 'These people come near to me with their mouth and honor me with their lips, but their hearts are far from me'" (Isa. 29:13). In many ways, God describes what normal so-called Christians look like today. He says, "They are not close to me at all. They talk the God talk, but their hearts and their actions are not anywhere near me."

As God looks at many of us living on the earth today, I imagine that's exactly how he would describe us. We're not much different from those who aren't Christians. We're normal. We spend our time and our money like normal people. We behave like most others. We have the same problems in our marriages, and with our kids, that people around us have.

The divorce rate for Christians is no lower than for non-Christians. We may claim to believe in God, but we don't want to believe so much that it makes us different. We don't want to go overboard with this whole religion thing. Sure, we want to believe in God, but we don't want to stand out and have others misunderstand and label us.

In the third chapter of Revelation, Jesus talks to seven churches. For six of them, although he corrects them, he at least has something good to say about each one. However, he offers nothing positive about the seventh one, the church of Laodicea. The severity of his warning makes more sense if you know a little about the place. Laodicea was a phenomenally wealthy city. Thirty-five years before these verses were written, Laodicea had been leveled by a massive earthquake. Because they were so affluent, they were able to rebuild immediately. Like most people who have the means, they didn't just rebuild what they had before. They rebuilt on a much larger, grander scale and ended up with a city much like we have today: huge theaters, gigantic stadiums, fancy public spas, and beautiful shopping centers. Imagine the Strip in Las Vegas materializing overnight, and you're not far from what it must have been like to watch the rebirth of this ancient pleasure capital. However, they paid a steep price. Between rebuilding their amazing cityscape and enjoying its new amenities, they forgot about God. Sure, they believed in him, acknowledged him, but he had nothing to do with how they lived.

So here's what Jesus had to say to them: "I know your deeds, that you are neither cold nor hot. I wish you were either one or the other!" (Rev. 3:15). Notice that he says "I know your deeds" and not "I've heard your words" or "I appreciate what you say." Nope, it's as clear as the crystal chandeliers hanging from their ceilings. Jesus says, "I know your actions, your works, how you behave." And his message is just as clear: "I know you claim to believe in me, but I don't see it in the way you live."

They weren't coldhearted haters of God who wanted nothing to do with following Jesus and his teachings. They weren't turned off to the things of God. But they weren't hot-blooded, passionate pursuers of God either. They weren't on fire, burning with a desire to know him, love him, and serve him. They were just kind of … there. Trucking down the wide-open road, going along their merry way. Just like everyone else. Just like normal.

Another historical fact helps us appreciate Jesus' words. Although Laodicea was a very wealthy city, they didn't have a reliable local source of water that could support their population. So they had to bring in all of their water from two sources. One, a hot spring, could be piped in, but by the time the water arrived, it had cooled considerably and become tepid. The other water source was a cold stream some miles away. By the time it reached the city, it had warmed up to room temperature. So Laodicea didn't have hot water, and they didn't have cold water — only lukewarm.

"So, because you are lukewarm — neither hot nor cold — I am about to spit you out of my mouth" (Rev. 3:16). The Greek word translated as "spit you out" is *emeo*. It means literally to spew, to spit, or to vomit. (You knew I'd find a way to get back to this, didn't you?) Jesus charges, "You should know who I am, but you're no different from everyone else. I can't stomach you. You make me want to hurl."

Imagine God looking at most of what passes for Christianity today and saying, "I know who I am. I know what I've done for you. I sent you my Son, Jesus, so that you could truly live. And yet you act like you think that simply squeezing me into your schedule every now and then will satisfy me — the one and only true, holy God."

THE ULTIMATE OXYMORON

An oxymoron is two words that are opposites blended together. Jumbo shrimp. Government efficiency. Microsoft Works. If there is one oxymoron that is above all others, I'd argue it is lukewarm Christian. What *is* a lukewarm Christian? It could be described as someone who believes in Christ but is no different from people who don't.

To be a disciple of Jesus, to be one of his, means to die to ourselves and to live holy unto him. How can we be halfhearted about the one who bled and died and rose again so we could know God? How can we call Christ our Lord and yet live as though he doesn't even exist? Lukewarm Christian? There shouldn't be such a thing. It makes God want to vomit.

When I read about the people of Laodicea, I can't help thinking of our world. The stadiums, the theaters, the malls. It's so similar to theirs. It's easy to believe in God in our country. It's almost more difficult to serve him genuinely when our lives are so easy.

In other places in the world, it's just the reverse. Because there's such a steep price for following Jesus, there's no choice but to live a radically different life. There's no way to be lukewarm in such cultures. Do you want to see where the church of Jesus is hot? Do you want to see some fire? Visit a country where, if you confess Christ, you'll go to prison or even be executed. In those places, if you call yourself a Christian, it means something — *everything*. Identifying yourself as a Christian can literally cost you your life. These followers of Jesus are forced to sacrifice. They give. They pray. They're different. They *really* believe.

It's harder here in our country, where you can sort of believe and still blend in. This is the basis for my concern: you can be lukewarm and not even know it. Worse yet, you may know it ... and not care.

Maybe you feel like you have enough of God as long as the economy is okay. Honestly, even in a slow economy, we're still rich. As we talked about earlier, people who live a normal life have all their basic needs met as well as the riches of opportunities denied to those truly impoverished. Yet we still want to be richer. Because if we are, we don't need God. Anything we need we can design, build, or buy.

This is the same message Jesus drives home to the Laodiceans: "You say, 'I am rich; I have acquired wealth and do not need a thing.' But you do not realize that you are wretched, pitiful, poor, blind and naked" (Rev. 3:17). Is there such a thing as a lukewarm Christian? Can those words go together? I'm not sure. This passage doesn't sound like it. Wretched. Pitiful. Poor. Blind. Naked. The prodigal son's father didn't say, "Praise God! My son who was blind is still blind!" No. He said, "This son of mine was dead and is alive again; he was lost and is found" (Luke 15:24). Clearly, you can't be lukewarm and still be eligible for that full life Jesus said he came to give us (John 10:10).

TURN UP THE WEIRD

There is hope. The Laodiceans claimed to believe in Christ, but they were lukewarm. God was about to spit them out. But just a few verses later, in Revelation 3:19 – 22, Jesus says, "Those whom I love I rebuke and discipline. So be earnest, and repent. Here I am! I stand at the door and knock. If anyone hears my voice and opens the door, I will come in and eat with him, and he with me. To him who overcomes, I will give the right to sit with me on my throne, just as I overcame and sat down with my Father on his throne. He who has an ear, let him hear what the Spirit says to the churches."

Can *you* hear what he's saying?

He said he's knocking. He said *if* you hear his voice, and *if* you'll open the door, only then will he come in. But he's not in yet. If you've been lukewarm, if you've been normal or comfortable, he's knocking on your door. He wants you to let him in — all the way in. He desperately wants you to know him. So many people believe in God, but they don't really know him. And because they don't really know him, they are lukewarm. The truth is, if you truly knew him, you couldn't be lukewarm or halfhearted. If you remain lukewarm, maybe it's because you don't know who God really is.

Jesus is the Alpha and the Omega. He is the Beginning and the End. He is the First and the Last. He said, "I am the true vine," "I am the door," "I am the gate," "I am the way, the truth, and the life," "I am the bread of life," "I am the good shepherd." Who is he? He is the one who was humble enough to come riding on a donkey. And yet, when he returns, he will be riding a white horse, wearing a robe dipped in blood. On his thigh will be written, "The King of kings and the Lord of lords." Out of his mouth will come a sword with which to judge the nations. He is the lion and he is the lamb of God. He is the one who was without sin, born in a cave, so that no one would ever feel too low for him. Yet he called the religious people a brood of vipers. They didn't get him. He told the sinners, "I love you." He told the rich it would be hard for them to enter the kingdom of God. He is the one who was beaten and bled and suffered and died and rose again — so that we could have life.

When you know him and when you recognize all that you've been forgiven, it changes everything. You cannot be the same. His power sets you free. His power forgives you, and all of a sudden you cannot be lukewarm. You *have* to tell people about him because of all that he's done in your life. You can't contain him. You can't keep him to yourself. You're not that selfish. He has changed you. You'll want others to know so badly that you won't care what people think. You'll care only what he thinks, because you'll understand that he's your audience of one. He's not just your Savior. He is your Lord, the King of kings of your life. Your life is no longer your own, but his. You'll live only for him.

When you know him and follow after him, this world no longer feels like your home. You find yourself more uncomfortable being normal and more comfortable being weird. You realize that the things of this world will burn away. No one wants to be foolish enough to sell out for something that won't last.

Instead, you're heavenly-minded. You set your mind on things above. Because of that, you're radically generous. You see your money and possessions as tools for you to use to advance his kingdom, to bring glory to him. When you do sin, you repent. You want to change. But it's not because you're afraid he might not forgive you. You know there's no condemnation for those who are in Christ Jesus. No, you hate to disappoint him, and you hate to live in the low life of sin.

You are different because you've been changed. You don't have the same values everyone else does. Because you *know* him. Your heart aches for those who don't know him. Your heart is no longer so tied up in the strings of the world. You find meaning and identity and purpose by losing yourself in service to others.

But let me warn you. When you escape normal and become a person who is God's kind of weird, some people will make fun of you. Don't worry when they do. That's part of following Christ. The only time you should worry is when no one makes fun of you. If you're normal, no one will.

If you have just enough of Christ to satisfy you but not enough to change you, answer his knock and let him make himself at home with you.

If you have just enough of Christ to satisfy you but not enough to change you, answer his knock and let him make himself at home with you.

You've purposefully chosen to leave the broad path. You're gladly traveling the narrow road. Your journey may seem weird to others, but your destination will be infinitely better than anything a settle-for-normal world can offer.

Because you can't settle for normal any longer. You can't be normal, because

238

CONCLUSION

you are getting to know the loving, grace-filled, all-powerful God of the universe. And as you come to know him, you're becoming like him. The more you are like him, the more different you will be.

Weird.

Notes

1. These results are from a 2009 study conducted by the Nielsen-funded Council for Research Excellence and by Ball State University's Center for Media Design (Council for Research Excellence, "Ground-Breaking Study of Video Viewing Finds Younger Boomers Consume More Video Media Than Any Other Group," March 26, 2009, *www.researchexcellence.com/news/032609_vcm.php*).

2. Tim Keller, *Counterfeit Gods* (New York: Dutton, 2009), 171.

3. Many of the ideas in this chapter came from Andy Stanley's message series titled "How to Be Rich." To obtain a copy, you can go to *northpoint.org*. I'm trying to talk Andy into writing a book on this subject. If he does, buy it!

4. *www.cnbc.com/id/32862851/More_Upper_Income_Workers_Living_Paycheck_to_Paycheck*.

5. Lillian Kwon, "Survey: Churches Losing Youths Long Before College," *Christian Post*, June 29, 2009, *www.christianpost.com/article/20090629/survey-churches-losing-youths-long-before-college/index.html*.

6. *http://www.usatoday.com/life/television/news/2010-01-20-sexcov20_CV_N.htm*.

7. "Statistics and Information on Pornography in the USA," *Blazing Grace.org*, *www.blazinggrace.org/cms/bg/pornstats* (accessed October 2010).

LIFECHURCH.TV

Looking for a LifeChurch near you?
For campus locations and service times, visit:
www.lifechurch.tv

- - -

Worship online from anywhere!
Join the online community.

With more than 50 service times during the week,
Church Online makes it easy:
www.live.lifechurch.tv

- - -

Download the Bible to your mobile device or access it online at:
www.YouVersion.com/download

The free online Bible that will revolutionize the way
you interact with God's Word.

Search for "Bible" on iTunes

OPEN
LIFECHURCH.TV

FREE church resources.
Sermons, graphics, kids curriculum and more!

www.open.lifechurch.tv